HOW
CULTURE
WORKS

HOW
CULTURE
WORKS

PAUL BOHANNAN

THE FREE PRESS

NEW YORK LONDON TORONTO SYDNEY TOKYO SINGAPORE

The Free Press
A Division of Simon & Schuster Inc.
866 Third Avenue, New York, N.Y. 10022

Printed in the United States of America

printing number

1 2 3 4 5 6 7 8 9 10

Library of Congress Cataloging-in-Publication Data

Bohannan, Paul.
    How culture works / Bohannan.
      p. cm.
    Includes bibliographical references and index.
    ISBN 0-02-904505-3
    1. Culture. 2. Social behavior in animals.   I. Title.
HM101.B6319 1995
306—dc20   94–31733
                                                                 CIP

There's no limit
to how complicated things can get
on account of
one thing leading to another
—E. B. WHITE

Contents

Road Map

For well over a hundred years, *culture* has been a substantive—a noun. It either did things or things happened to it. It existed, but it was inert.

The call has been made by many to examine culture as a process. The call—and little more. The callers don't go on to tell you how to do that.

Culture does not have a useful companionate verb[1], as *life* has its cognate, *to live*. Leslie White tried to supply it, but what he did was turn the noun *culture* into the verb "to culture." He didn't have any takers. In part, he was ahead of his time. But he had an even greater strike against him: he tried to use the word as a variant of itself.

In the present exercise, *culture* is a verb more in the conceptual than in the grammatical sense. I have found the word *culturize* useful in some places in this book, but its meaning is restricted; certainly it does not provide an analogy to the *life/live* situation.

Two assumptions underlie this exercise:

- there is a time dimension to all culture, and
- one state of culture often leads to another (in ways that do not, as well as ways that do, imply cultural evolution).

I am beginning with something as simple as a flowchart, a process that is today followed by many computer programmers to assist in planning the timing and flow of projects. As far as I am aware, the first flowchart in anthropology was that given by Arnold van Gennep in 1908.[2] As far as I know, no others were added until 1957, when both Victor Turner[3] and I[4] came up with flowcharts. Michael Thompson introduced some interesting and more complex ones in 1979.[5] I built on it preliminarily in 1984.[6]

There is one additional set of ideas on which I build: that of the *cultural trap*, which as far as I know was introduced by John Platt.[7] The proposition is this: culture is adaptive—that is, it facilitates human use of and participation in the environment—until the context changes so that it is no longer adaptive. When that happens, culture may become a trap and may even lead to disaster.[8] For example, if agricultural methods that ruin the soil are pursued without change, those agricultural methods become a cultural trap; if they are not altered the whole culture–environment arrangement will break down. Just so, ideas of law or government that work for communities of a few hundred people must be changed when the same communities grow to several hundred thousand and their family and religious pressures no longer assure social equity.

The history of the world can be seen as the study of cultural processes: those that create adjustments to changed environmental conditions on the one hand, and those that lead to cultural traps on the other. Some cultural traps (like power struggles as we hand over offices) have been overcome, at least in some places. Others (like ethnicity) have not. We are surrounded today by culture traps, as every cultural tradition has always been surrounded by such traps. Only if we recognize those traps, which means understanding the way our actions and our beliefs turn into traps, and actively seek exits or solutions or both, can our civilization survive.

Ancient Greek civilization foundered on a social trap. Having invented the city-state, the Greeks stuck to their guns and could not take the next step: agreeing on ways for city-states to cooperate and coexist. Communist civilization ended in a social trap very like it: having invented a new form of planned economy, they were unable to adapt it to changing world conditions, particularly to the information revolution.

But, what about us? Do we know enough about social and cultural process to avoid the traps?

In an important sense, this book is about recognizing and avoiding cultural traps—which, here, include the traps of social organization. We cannot avoid these traps without understanding just how we (like everybody else) walk into them. Anthropology and the other social sciences know enough today so that we should be able to get on with the job. The secret is in simplifying what we know to the point where we can apply our knowledge successfully and people will not confuse our applying it with political manipulation.

Works of social science can be ranked along a scale from simple to obfuscating. Obfuscating is easier. I have tried hard to be simple in this book. Sometimes simple spills over into simplistic or obvious. But restating the obvious in a new context sometimes clears the air.

The gravest need in social science is a good program of synthesis. We know a lot. There is an awful lot of theory out there, some of it even good. There are libraries of good ethnography, many of them all but unread.

But systematic synthesis of what we know is in short supply. Transferring insights from one realm to another so that our whole enterprise can become less fragmented is a worthwhile goal. It can be achieved only by gaining simplicity. We need ways to get our initial premises as clear as our subsequent logic, and to make simple, clear statements about how it all fits together.

And it is only with such synthesis that we can recognize cultural traps and begin to overcome them. In this book, I ask how culture works. It is akin to the medical profession asking how the human body works.

HOW
CULTURE
WORKS

Part I

Culture in the Natural World

Culture is as natural as life. We shortchange ourselves if we view culture as artifice to be opposed to nature. On the other hand, we must separate cultural information from genetic information. The two are in no sense opposed; indeed, the confusion arises because they are so totally commingled in our experience. In the course of growing up, we learn culture as ways to exercise our genetic capacities.

We cannot deal with culture as long as we oppose it to nature rather than accept it as an integral part of nature, or as long as we confuse it with our genetic endowment (which some biologists still do) or with God's will (which some fundamentalists of all faiths always have).

When we finally learn to deal with culture as part of the natural world, but a part separable from our biology, we can question it, ask how it works, take advantage of parts of it, and learn to avoid some of its manifestations, just as we deal with any other natural phenomenon.

Chapter 1

Matter, Life, and Culture

People are subject to constraints that arise from the rules of matter, the rules of life, and the rules of culture. Matter is what everything in the universe is made of, including us—the elemental constituents of human bodies follow the rules of chemistry and physics. Until life is added, matter is inert.

The biological condition imbues matter with qualities that are absent in nonliving matter. Life is a way of organizing matter. It transforms matter, but does not in the least affect the principles according to which matter works.

Living matter can be transformed yet again—by culture. Culture transcends and enriches matter and life but does not change the way physics, chemistry, or biology work. Culture emerges from life just as life emerges from matter.

The rules of culture are extensions of the rules of matter and life, just as the rules of life are extensions of the rules of matter. If the rules of matter failed to apply, we could not exist, even as rocks. If the rules of life did not apply, we would be inert. Dead. And if the rules of culture did not apply, we would be exiled from the abundant world we know—without tools and without meanings. Like dinosaurs.

3

Scientists know a lot about the physics and chemistry of matter. Not enough, of course, but quite a bit. Scientists are fast learning a lot about biology. Not yet enough, but the human genome will be mapped within a few years, which is taking biology to a new level.

We know a lot less about culture. But we know enough to begin to define a set of rules that it follows, just as surely as matter follows its rules (discovered by physicists and chemists and geologists), or as living things follow their rules (discovered by biologists). The rules of culture are far more complex and infinitely more abstract and subtle than the rules of physics or biology, subtle and difficult though those may be. Worst of all, the search for the rules of culture is hampered by the irony that people cannot even think about culture except through the categories of thought that we have learned from the culture we grew up in and the one in which we have been trained. We must make gigantic efforts to step outside our culture-laden views. We must struggle to examine our own culture in the same framework as every other culture. But of course we can examine other cultures much more easily, because we can see their differences from our own. It is every anthropologist's conviction that if we can see many views at the same time, we may be able to transcend the limited view of culture that is allowed us by any single culture, including our own.

Alfred Kroeber in 1917 used what at one level would seem to be the very apt word *superorganic* to refer to the cultural realm.[1] However, the problems anthropologists faced in 1917 were far different from our own—his long article deals with the inclination of many late-nineteenth- and early-twentieth-century scholars to give biological answers to what, it was becoming clear, were actually cultural questions and to distinguish race, language, and culture.

Life, to sum up, adds processes to the way matter works. And culture adds further processes that refine the processes of living matter. Several traps are already evident:

• Separating culture from life, which Boas and Kroeber were able to do, does not mean that the two are in totally different realms and certainly not that culture can override biological requirements and laws.

• It is true that cultural evolution is the means by which acquired characteristics can be "inherited." Because culture is malleable, as life forms are not (or were not until the ongoing genetic revolution), it is easy to overestimate the malleability of culture as compared to life. Seeing the way biological evolution and cultural evolution interlink remains a major problem in our own day.

All scientists (even physicists) deal with all three kinds of processes: the processes of matter, those of life, and those of culture. Physicists are as limited by their culture (for example, in selecting problems or when challenged by wrong-headed assumptions within their culture) as anyone else. Any scientist can, of course, create a specific problem or set of problems that excludes one, or even two, of these trouble spots. But the scientist must learn not to sneak in by the back door those very premises and ideas that he has thrown out the front door. Those scientists who get caught in the trap of taking for granted their "objectivity" and who think that they have "overcome" their biases are ripe for letting those very biases slip unconsciously into the structures of their problems or into the way they read their results. Every scientist who announces the results of his or her investigations thereby inserts them into a human context—and had better read his or her culture and biology as clearly as his or her physics. The fact that the culture and the biology were not stated in the problem does not mean that they are not present in it.

Matter is difficult to define because there is nothing more basic to reduce it to. Life, being even more difficult to define, was at one time called "a mystery." Defining culture has proved all but impossible. Yet we know what culture is, just as we know what life and matter are. All three are what we might call rock-bottom perceptions—they cannot be definitionally simplified.

THE BOUNDARY BETWEEN MATTER AND LIFE

If we focus on the categories *matter* and *life*, we can readily understand the distinction between living things like trees and birds and nonliving things like rock. However, if we focus on the boundary between the quick and the inert, problems arise. Viruses exist more or less on that boundary—they are inert substances until they drift inside a living cell, whereupon they take on some of the qualities of living things. Just so, difficulties emerge when we focus on the boundary between *life* and *culture*. Woodpecker finches in the Galapagos use what we can only call a tool to dig grubs out of holes in trees. Is that culture?

The special characteristics of living things are easy to grasp.

• *Living things are, first of all, feedback systems*. They experience their environment as stimuli, and then adapt to those stimuli.

• *Living things metabolize*. They absorb substances from the environment, turn parts of them into usable energy, and expel the rest back into the environment.

• *Living things move*. Sap mounts the stems of plants; flowers open and close. Sponges circulate seawater within themselves to extract nutrients. At the other extreme, caribou migrate. Some migratory birds travel as much as 20,000 miles each year. Human beings have become globe-trotters, now on the verge of spacefaring.

• *Living things grow*. They begin as germs or seeds. By predictable processes of growth, they increase in size and acquire specialized functions. Matter is eternal, although it may be turned into energy and back again. Life, on the other hand, is a collection of many lives. Every life has a beginning and an end, for all that life itself goes on.

• *Living things can reproduce*. Reproduction may take place sexually or asexually—bacteria reproduce asexually, plants such as geraniums can grow from slips (but, it can be argued, that is not reproduction strictly speaking); female lizards of some species in harsh environmental circumstances are capable of asexual reproduction, creating what amount to clones of themselves.

These five characteristics define life—biologists may wish to add others, but none will deny these. A visual summary, as in Figure 1–1, is helpful; it also helps to give us the feel of flowcharts.

FIGURE 1–1

Matter Turns into Life

THE BOUNDARY BETWEEN LIFE AND CULTURE

The characteristics of the life/culture border are even more complex than those of the matter/life border. They seem to be structured as a chain, even a pyramid. Each characteristic joins the characteristics of its own foundation to become the foundation for subsequent links.

Behavior is a basic link that can be added to the life chain as it stretches toward culture. Again, its boundaries are vague. The movement of a heliotropic plant as it turns toward the sun is certainly movement. But is it behavior? Most animals have specialized organs in order to achieve various kinds of behavior such as walking or communicating. Obviously it is a matter of definition. The line between mere reflex and behavior cannot be defined, except pedantically. Anybody who tries instantly makes a pedant of himself, and just as instantly will be refuted by somebody with a different flavor of pedantry. That is called academic life.

Learning is the next advance. Cultureless creatures like insects get all the information required for their behavior from their genes; in the language of computer science, they are said to be "hardwired." For them no learning is involved, only certain environmental conditions are required. A tick can remain on grass or other vegetation until the right stimulus is perceived—usually the odor and temperature of a living animal. The tick attaches itself to the passing animal and its life course continues. Neither learning nor conscious awareness is required to be a successful tick— and so ticks have no culture.

Learning is a process of perceiving and then repeating some modes of behavior that enhance life. The capacity to learn is often superadded to behavior in the animal kingdom. Like behavior or movement, its several characteristics may be present separately, but one way to define *learning* is to say that these characteristics must all be present at the same time.

Because it involves perception, learning is one aspect of a feedback mechanism, which may in fact be a hierarchical series of feedbacks, in which the results of the lower stratum form the comparator for the next higher stratum.[2] Some animals have more layers in their learning mechanism than others. For example, birds like the mockingbird learn to sing a wide variety of songs and keep learning new songs throughout their lives. Other birds learn some songs, but only during a limited period of time, after which their repertory is set. Still other birds don't learn songs at all—they sing out of their hard wiring. Any bird's capacity to learn songs is governed by the information in its genes. Primates, and especially human beings, are especially good at learning.

Choice may be added to the repertoire of abilities by a subset of those who learn. Many animals have the capacity to make choices—they must, at some points in their lives, choose one path instead of another if they are to behave at all. Their decision as to which path they take determines their fate.

Choice can be constrained in many ways: by the nature of the purposes to be served, by the conditions of a specific environment, or by the demands of other members of the same species or of other species in the environment. Among human beings, so much capacity to choose has been introduced into the hard wiring that sometimes the hard wiring seems (falsely) to have disappeared.

Culture, finally, may be superadded once behavior, learning, and choice are in position. Culture is a combination of the tools and the meanings that expand behavior, extend learning, and channel choice. The experiences of one animal can, with culture, be made useful to neighbors and descendants. A cultured animal like a human being, when faced with a choice, is likely to have some information about the probable results of each of the options.

However, there is more to it. The young of many birds and mammals are instructed by their elders. Bluebirds appear to teach their young to fly, not just to encourage them to have a go. Cats learn hunting techniques from their mothers. But cultured species can transmit information to one another even more effectively: because they have an external store of information on which to draw.

Culture is like a prosthesis—it allows the creature to extend its capacities and to do things that its specialized body cannot otherwise do. Chimpanzees are not genetically equipped to get termites out of their mounds, although all of them like to eat termites (as do some human beings). Chimps can, however, make termite-fishing sticks to do it. The stick is a cultural extension of the chimpanzee. It is a tool. Before Jane Goodall discovered chimpanzees making tools, culture was usually said to be the prerogative of human beings. But now either we had to stop defining culture by mere tool use or else we had to extend the idea of culture to other creatures. Then, when those Galapagos woodpecker finches were also discovered using tools, it became obvious that some signs of culture—simple tools—may be far more widespread than the original definers of culture had ever dreamed.

Human beings are hardwired to learn culture; nevertheless all culture is learned. Not a single piece of culture anywhere is itself hardwired into people. Human choices are made, within the limits of hardwired reflexes, on the basis of the biological capacities to choose and act, as well as on the culture-based capacity to reason.

Culture is indeed tools. But it is also meaning. And that fact complicates the definition of culture. The immense human capacity for choice leads to many different satisfactory solutions to the challenges of living. Not unlimited solutions, but an immense number. An act can have a different meaning in different contexts or to different peoples. Where do the apes and woodpecker finches fit in now?

The cultural meanings instilled in human beings standardize their choices just as readily, but not as unalterably, as hardwiring. People, when they are young, learn that some edible substances are food while others are not. They can extend and alter what they define as food by choice or necessity; nevertheless some people will flatly refuse to eat perfectly edible things because they have not previously defined them as food. (Being an anthropologist requires that you be able to eat anything edible that is put in front of you—but some of them won't.)

Such cultural limiting carries some risk. Limiting our choices may undermine or even disallow our human—indeed, our animal—capacity to choose. Such limits impose a sort of unchosen choice. Whenever a cultural tradition rules out the inclination or the right to choose, the result may save time, provide security, and create a group of like-minded creatures—however, it can also lead to catastrophe. For example, specific standardizations of choice may not work if the environmental situation changes—if weather patterns change, you have to give up old choices and turn to new ones. If the policies of governments change, we may have to give up a lot of old ways. Whenever we do not leave the way open for learning to change our prescribed choices, our specific cultural directives can become as great a handicap as saber teeth were to Oligocene tigers when their environment changed—and what had been a positive adaptation became a deadly handicap.

We are in the realm of irony. Cultural standards that in past times were positive adjustments *may* lose their advantage when things change—indeed, with change in either the physical or the social environment old cultural ways can work against the very people they were devised over the generations to help.

Culture can be used to coerce others; most often today such coercion is called prejudice or ethnocentrism. But a new government can make a people change their religion. Or a coercive community can expel members who take on "newfangled" cultural ways—the "old-time religion is good enough for me" syndrome.

Culture can go haywire, particularly if its principles are taken to what seem to be logical conclusions that are nevertheless based on inadequate or erroneous premises. The prescriptions of a culture can reach the point where people overlook new possibilities for improvement because their old premises may not be questioned. The Aztecs were conquered as much by their own myths—which told them that they were living in the last of five worlds and that total destruction was on the way—as by the *conquistadores*.

Questioning premises that we do not know we hold is not easy. Before Copernicus, people did not know that they held the kind of ideas about the structure of the universe that we today associate with Ptolemy; they were convinced that their old perceptions of the earth, sun, and moon were "correct." It took centuries for Copernicus's ideas to be generally accepted.

Examining one's premises is a skill. But examining our unconscious premises means that we must first find a way to become aware that they are there. Only if we first learn what the premises of our standardized cultures are can we evaluate them. In other words, we have to get past our own cultural limits if we are to examine our enduring problems anew and hence make new choices about them. Questioning old premises creates discomfort both in ourselves and in the people around us. We are usually loath to do it, even when we know how. To examine premises, we must first realize that we have them. Then we must reassure ourselves that we and the social order will both survive when they are questioned.

The precise point at which life appears in matter is difficult to discern. The point at which culture is imparted to life is equally difficult; Figure 1–2 can only suggest it. But one thing we can be sure of: just as life may create hazards that may lead to its extinction, culture creates hazards for the creatures who bear it. How many faulty premises do we logically build on that then lead us to undesirable ends? Just as mortality is built into life, so absurdity is built into culture.

AND WHAT ABOUT SOCIETY?

Many—indeed, most—creatures of the animal kingdom use the principles of society much as people use tools; social organization

FIGURE 1–2
How Life Acquires Culture

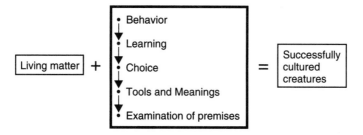

allows the members of any species to do many things they could not do any other way. Animals, having sense organs, react to what they perceive. When another creature is in their environment, it is perceived as part of that environment. When two creatures are each in the environment of the other, and when each makes a behavioral adaptation to the presence of the other, a social situation has formed—indeed, the dyad of two individuals is the basic unit of society.

There at least two other determinants of sociality: first of all, since resources are scarce, competition and aggression are built in—and those are social relationships. Moreover, since life has mortality built in, it also requires reproduction. Two sexes developed as a way for both plants and animals to carry out reproduction. Copulation is the mode of sexual reproduction of most (not all) animals more complex than oysters. Therefore, a social dimension to animal life, based on sexuality, has to be assumed.

Society precedes culture. Some form of sociality is to be found in most (not all) species of animals. It thus may be affected by culture somewhat as other aspects of living are affected by it—we shall examine the way culture affects sociality in Chapters 3 and 4. Then in Chapter 8 we shall return to the subject, because sociality is essential in understanding biological and cultural rhythms. Here we have only defined the most basic terms of inquiry, but society and the impact of culture on it will come up many times in this book.

Chapter 2

A Model of the Human Animal

People are very good at culture. Indeed they have, in their evolution, specialized in culture much as bloodhounds have specialized in odors or dolphins have specialized in water sports. We are what we are because we are cultured. However, that is no excuse to lose sight of the fact that, for all that cultural specialization, there is an animal inside each of us—and an associated fact: culture, although it cannot override animality, can stretch it and do funny things with it.

People (and all other animals) work like thermostats. As you drive down the road, you constantly adjust your car's trajectory to keep it in the correct lane and moving at the correct speed. You judge both lane and speed by signals you constantly pick up from the surface of the road—from other cars, people, stray dogs, junk on the road, and from the way the car is running. You correct to a standard: when you were young, you learned to drive on the right side of the road (or the left, if you grew up in Great Britain, Thailand, New Zealand, India, or Japan). You also learned something about speed limits and the function of red and green traffic lights, to which you learned to correct the movement of your car. You have learned to do all this so well that most of it is no longer conscious.

But people are not *mere* thermostats. Indeed, they are so complex that it took decades to figure out that they—and other animals too—are feedback mechanisms working like thermostats. Their complexity increases whenever they change their own settings.

WHY DO WE BEHAVE?

Early in the twentieth century, psychologists developed a stimulus–response model of behavior. The basic premise of the model was that a stimulus external to an animal "causes" it to respond—that is, to behave. This basic premise is correct but inadequate, because it denies intention in the behaving animal. It further assumes what we know to be untrue: that all stimuli felt by the person or animal come from outside. Hunger, lust, pain—these and other stimuli can come from within the organism and can be among the strongest stimuli we know.[1]

Critics of the stimulus–response model pointed out that there was a feeling, thinking, learning organism, be it a rat or a person, in the middle there somewhere. The animal lives between the stimulus and the response; but that animal is no passive black box. It has intentions. Further, an animal's response may be to do nothing—to *not* behave. Thus *response* and *behavior* are not the same thing. The complex nature of the environment that supplies some of the stimuli also changes constantly unless it is controlled by an experimenter. *Environment* and *stimulus* must also thus be separated. Figure 2–1 can be read: (1) the environment gives rise to (2) a stimulus perceived by (3) the organism, which (4) responds—and which may [but may not] (5) behave; its behavior (6) alters the stimulus, and (7) may alter the environment.

In the 1970s, several psychologists put forward the idea that the organism is a servomechanism. The most satisfying discussion of this point is to be found in Powers's book called *Behavior, the Control of Perception*.[2] The title states the basic premise: the behaving animal has a purpose, which is to affect and control its stimulus (Arrow 6 in Figure 2–1). Thus, we have to examine both the components of a feedback mechanism and the results, in the environment, of the behavior that emerges.

FIGURE 2–1

A Modified Stimulus–Response Diagram

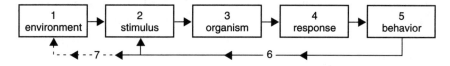

Every thermostat is set so that within a limited range of stimuli, no response is called for. That is, the stimulus is "right" when it is within that range. The rightness is measured by a device called a comparator. Sticking with the thermostat analogy, a comparator is a strip made up of sheets of two different metals welded together that respond differently to temperature change.

The comparator correlates the actual stimulus against the desirable range. When the measured phenomenon—in our analogy, the temperature—falls within the range set by the comparator, nothing happens. However, when the stimulus exceeds or falls below the limits set by the comparator, a signal is sent that something should happen. With that signal, be it "too much" or "too little," the thermostat—or the animal—does something to bring the stimulus back into the preset sphere. The thermostat turns the furnace on or off. The stimulus causes the animal to behave—it does something to change the stimulus.

The basic setting of any animal's comparator—including the human animal's—is genetic. It is "given" at the beginning of an individual life. By the working of evolutionary development, a creature is born "knowing" when some stimuli are "right." Insofar as a creature's response is innate instead of learned, it is a genetic deposit in that creature's knowledge bank.

However, many animals superadd another kind of rightness awareness to that genetic one: learned rightness awareness. Within the constraints set by the genetic endowment, some of the options can be elaborated by learning. Young crows, when they first leave the nest, learn to judge whether a branch will support their weight; it takes them two or three days. The animal learns *how* to behave—what to do to bring the stimulus within the desired bounds. For better or for worse, it has learned from experience.

Thus behavior not only affects the stimulus, it also leaves a residue of experience in the behaving organism that is likely to redefine or even change the standards within the comparator. That is the learning deposit in the knowledge bank.

Genetic information and learned information, once deposited, are commingled. These processes are summarized in Figure 2–2, which can be read: a situation arises in (E) the environment which (O) the organism, i.e., the individual person, perceives as (S) a stimulus. The stimulus, detected by the animal's (A) acceptor system (its senses), is thrown against (C) a comparator whose standards are determined by genetics and experience. The resulting (R) response may [but may not] lead to (B) behavior designed to alter the stimulus, and may [but may not] take the path of altering the environment. Anyone who wants to read this process as the learning aspect amalgamating with and expanding the genetic aspect can do so, but be warned: doing so makes it easy to give unwarranted primacy to the genetic. The genetic provides both capacity and limitation; in that sense—but only in that sense—it also provides a foundation.

The most interesting aspect of all this is the flow. Much, but certainly not all, of the stimulus originates in the environment—the rest (S' on the chart) originates in the workings of the body, com-

FIGURE 2–2

The Individual's Stimulus–Behavior–Learning Loop

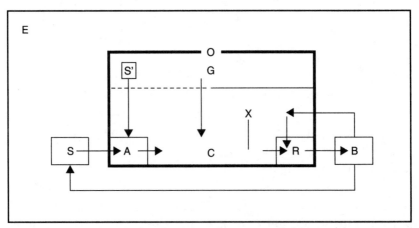

(E = environment; O = organism; G = genetic endowment; X = experience; S = stimulus;
S' = internal stimuli; A = acceptor system; C = comparator; R = response; B = behavior)

ing to us as pain or emotion. An external stimulus is perceived by means of an "acceptor system"—sense organs like the ears, eyes, and skin. Reactions to that stimulus filter through the comparator, a combination of nerves and the brain, where it is compared to all the combined (G) genetic and (X) experiential information in the bank (that is, $G + X$ in Figure 2–2). Any response, thus, leads simultaneously to more experiential information in the bank and to behavior that both changes the stimulus and reinforces or increases experience. In just this way, our experience is simultaneously enlarged by the range of possible options and limited by the choices we in fact make.

The next time a similar stimulus is perceived, it is compared with the information internalized by decisions and actions from earlier experiences, and against genetic capacities and limitations. The creature either repeats the action it learned earlier or (if the results were deemed unsatisfactory) makes a specific effort not to repeat that action but rather to find a new solution.

Now, a human characteristic: an integral part of any person's environment is the culture of the surrounding people. Thus as the person perceives, makes his or her own choices, and behaves, that person cannot help learning the local version of culture. Human beings have complicated the learning level: among the learned information are to be found techniques and attitudes— tools and meaning. Thus, culture is both inside the perceiving and acting person and outside him in the forms of its manifestations in material items and the action of other people.

No human behavior, whether genetic or learned or some combination of the two, can occur without being culturally evaluated. Evaluation need not be conscious; much unconscious evaluation, too, is culture bound.

That added evaluation is what separates human behavior from mere animal behavior. It is impossible for human beings to perform any "animal" behavior without evaluating it. Nonetheless we still perform it. Misperceiving this point has led—and, too often, still leads—to the denial that human beings have an animal nature or to the absurd statement that our "instincts" have given way to culture—which they have not—although our culture does color all our instincts and therefore creates a difference between them and the instincts of noncultured animals.

GROWTH AND LEARNING

For human beings and all other animals, growth changes the genetic standards of the comparator in a predictable pattern. That is, the genetic dimensions of the comparator do not reflect the same standards for behavior at all stages of the life course. For human beings and some other animals, moreover, the experiential dimension is also changed each day as we grow older, learn more, and take on new social tasks. It is the nature of personal experience that it is constantly reevaluated by the person in the light of changes in the environment and of other experiences. Our past experiences obviously do not change—what happened, happened. But our evaluation of those experiences can change several times a day. Reworking our experience is a normal dimension of growth and maturation. It is similar to what psychoanalysts call "working through."

The learning person has to learn categories and systems into which to file this mass of information that is being learned. If we could not create and use such categories—theorists in cognitive anthropology and linguistics call them *schemata*—it would be impossible to absorb all the information that we learn. We would soon be swamped with information. Our culture provides such schemata.

One definition of *schemata* is Ronald Casson's: "Conceptual abstractions that mediate between stimuli received by the sense organs and behavioral responses"[3]—that is, as part of the comparator. The term *schemata* puts the comparator into the plural and gives it structure. Although some schemata, like nouns and verbs, are universal among human beings and a few may be peculiar to one individual, most are cultural and thus shared by some but not shared by all.

The grammar of any language is a schema—indeed, the grammar of our native language provides our basic schema. No naive speaker of any language knows that grammar exists—the discovery of grammar was a tremendous intellectual feat. (As far as we know, that discovery was first made several thousand years ago by an ancient Sanskrit scholar named Panini.) To this day, people have to be taught that grammar exists, in spite of the fact that they speak their native language grammatically (if not always meeting the grammatical standards championed by their English teachers). Grammar is an indispensable matrix for putting thought into communicable form. In accordance with the grammar of our language, we divide meaning into units that are recognizable by others who speak the same language. We then put the units into the "right" (that is, grammatical) order as we speak. We transform the units in accordance with a set of grammatical rules—we can change tenses, make plurals, and adjust verb endings or adjectival forms. The categories of grammar shape not only our speech but our thought. We may not always *think* in words; but to *express ourselves* in language—that is, to communicate meaning—we usually use words and grammar. When people communicate anything beyond the most basic animal perceptions such as fear or lust, they must do so within the schemata of the grammar of some language.

A deep irony—and trap—arises here: human beings cannot communicate even their simplest perceptions without communicating the cultural values that underlie and shape these perceptions. Even the grammar carries those values. Differences in cultural values between the sender of a message and its receiver can lead to a lot of difficulty.

Some aspects of grammar are common to all languages, presumably reflecting genetic proclivities of the human brain. All languages, for example, have nouns and verbs. But many other aspects are not universal. In the language of the Tiv, a Nigerian society, the terms for color are verbs instead of adjectives: Tiv do not say that something "is red," but that it "reds," a way of speaking that brings perception into line with physics if not with English idiom. The information can be readily translated, but the feeling is different. The schemata are different. In that same language, you do not drop something; rather, it "drops" you. Instead of saying, "I dropped it," you say, "it fell away from me." (That is weak English, but the point is that in the Tiv language—and culture—the action lies with the object, not with the speaker.)

To summarize, human behavior exhibits two elements simultaneously: on the one hand, it is biological, animal behavior; on the other hand, it is cultured, symbolic, learned behavior. Human beings are genetically equipped to learn—not just to learn but to learn the symbolic dimensions of culture. The cultural dimension of the schemata need not be coterminous with the total schemata—after all, we have all had the experience of knowing things we cannot verbalize or explain.

Because of the schemata, what we learn is no mere copy of external reality. The schemata thus *seem* to be part of reality. Once the schemata are in our experience, it becomes almost impossible to perceive "reality" (whatever that is) without the schemata. The irony is profound.

Another way of saying all this is: a "thought" is a schematically organized perception—it necessarily includes a cultural evaluation.

The schemata in the comparator thus work to file what we perceive into patterns we already know. When we sense new information, processes in the comparator set to work: we do the best we can to fit the new sense perception into our accustomed schematic patterns of perception. Then, on the basis of our amalgam of information, we behave. When that action is successful, there is no need to upset the pattern.

Three conditions limit the culture we learn.

1. People have real genetic differences in perceptual acuity. Some people are, apparently, tone-deaf; some are certainly color-blind. People who are not born with "a good ear" have far more difficulty learning and appreciating music than those who have one; it may take more effort to learn, but a lot can be learned. Just so, color-blind people can learn to distinguish red from green, at least in some contexts, by using secondary stimuli—in American culture red traffic lights are, after all, always either above or to the left of green lights.

2. A person can learn *only* what the cultural environment provides, no matter what the genetic program may be capable of. However, we may very well not learn everything that the environment provides. The fact that it is there to be learned does not imply that a person learns it. Some traditions deny or understress an aspect of the culture that is known but associated with some other social group.

3. A person must learn culture in accordance with the demands made by other people. Even at a very early age, different demands may be made on boys than on girls or on members of different classes—there are some things that adults will not allow children (or some children—say boys, or untouchables,

or princesses) to learn. Yet, most of us learn forbidden information that at least some people in our environment think we would be better off not knowing—and we may go to a lot of trouble to stretch some of the parameters of our lives in order to learn it.

One result of all this learning and all these limiting conditions is immense variation among people, far beyond their genetic differences. Important, but often overlooked, is that the cultural component becomes more and more dominant as the person gets older, makes more choices, and gains more experience. Old people become more and more fully defined as just one of the many possibilities that were originally present in their genes. At the earliest ages of life, genetic endowment is paramount; in mid-life, cultural dimensions become more prominent. By old age, culture is almost overpowering. The differences among old persons are said by many gerontologists to be more stark than the differences at any earlier life stage. "Life experience particularizes us," as they put it.

The processes of learning culture thus make us human. It is ironic that the very same processes simultaneously make us provincial. In the process of learning culture, people come to regard the particular version of it that they learn—their own culture—as part of the natural world. Our most liberating human characteristics thus underlie our most imprisoning ones. In this sense, ethnocentrism is universal—and irony rules the world.

Chapter 3

What Culture Does to Society I

Culturized Animal Behavior

S ociety—living in a society—improves any species's prospects for ample food, ample protection, ample reproduction. Human beings have, in fact, been able to turn society into a sort of tool. All societies exist in a defining spatial context. The territorial juxtaposition of creatures, the way they exploit the territory, and their attachment to the territory lie at the foundation of any society.

Human beings share some of their basic social patterns with nonhuman animals. Most (not quite all) animals are social creatures. Human society looks different from animal society because people have culturized their social behavior—as, indeed, they have culturized all of their animal behavior. They have used culture to create principles of social organization beyond those found in animal society. Moreover different peoples, each faced with its own environment and each working toward its own goals, have culturized it in different ways. People have carried to a high art what early primatologists found baboons doing: adjusting their social organization to accommodate their numbers and to maximize their environment.

Human beings, like all individual animals, decide whether or not to associate with other specific members of their species. But they go on to do something else: they first create, and then preserve, the cultural tone and content of their associations. They do it in response to pressures from cultural environments added to pressures from the natural environment.

DYADS AND TRIADS

Although individual animals (including human beings) are indeed the *members* of their society, they are not the major *components* of that society.

- One person is the *behaving* unit, but
- the dyad of behaving persons is the basic *social* unit.

That is to say, society is composed of relationships and of compound structures of relationships—and only secondarily of individuals who are involved in relationships. When any creature finds another creature in the environment, one to which he or she must adapt, that second creature becomes a significant part of the environment of the first. The two creatures, each in the purview of the other, and each changing its behavior because of the presence and activities of the other, form the dyad. That dyad is a social relationship, the basic social component. When it is diagrammed, the basic unit looks something like the barbell in Figure 3–1.

Such "barbells" (each a social dyad) can be used, something like Tinker Toys, to build complex structures. Because each person may be in touch with many other people in the environment, the resulting structures can soon become quite complex. Moreover, a complex social structure may itself form a unit that becomes one pole of a larger dyad—that is, dyadic relationships can occur between groups. A given society may thus become very big and very complicated the very while that the principles underlying it remain simple.

FIGURE 3–1
A Dyad—The Basic Social Unit

Social dyads are effective when each of the two individuals (or two groups, or a group and an individual) either profits from association with the other or is not significantly harmed by the other. Although fear or cultural attitudes (often called "morality") sometimes do indeed lead to the survival of a dysfunctional or even destructive relationship, nevertheless the dyad usually disintegrates when its members cease to be valuable to one another. When the costs to one or both animals greatly exceed the rewards, or when the dyad is seriously beset by the envy of one toward the other, it is usually broken.

Problems that arise in the dyad are solved either by separation of the two parties (thus destroying the dyad), or by importing a third party and expanding the simple dyad into a triad.

A triad, the next most vital structure in society, is composed of three individuals and three dyads. Long ago, Harry Stack Sullivan noted that just as dyads may be beset by envy, triads can be beset by jealousy. The triad is found in the family; learning to deal with the social triad of mother/father/child is part of what Freud called the Oedipus complex. It is also found in international diplomacy. Jealousy within the triad may cause one party to withdraw or two parties to gang up on the third.

Each of the dyads in a triad is "refereed" by the third party. Such refereeing may sometimes lead to stability. For example, the NATO-Warsaw Pact-China triad of mutual distrust during the Cold War was quite stable. Each member monitored the relationship between the other two and adjusted accordingly. The absence of such a familiar triad in the days just after the Cold War was profoundly confusing to those involved in international relations. Indeed, the uncomfortable stability within the old diplomatic structure was fractured. As I write in 1994, no new stability has appeared.

An international corporation and a government can form a dyad, each being a "person" in the relationship. Pairs of spouses or whole families can interact with one another as dyads. However, when you add one more member, you get a new triad.

The triad itself may be reduced to a dyad whenever the parents, for example, combine their efforts in order to help or to discipline their child. That is to say, the two parents, joined together, form a single person vis-à-vis one or more of their children in a more inclusive dyad.[1]

FIGURE 3–2

A Dyad of Which One Pole Is Itself a Dyad

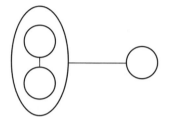

For example, the children may decide they want to spend the vacation at Disneyland; father wants to go fishing. Mother may join one or the other (forming a complex dyad) but she may figure out how they can do both.

Thus, once any social unit has more than three component dyads, it is almost always reduced to a simpler form—two interest groups (or groups defined in some other way) become the dyadic poles in the next more inclusive dyad.

These two forms—the dyad and the triad—provide the basics of social structure. They are thus the atoms of society. They work by hooking together in accordance with simple rules. Although the social system itself may become extremely complex, the principles remain simple.

Some animals alter their social structure seasonally; for example, deer form herds at certain times of the year, but they disaggregate into pairs at others, and are more or less solitary at still others. Human beings are more complex—they create interest groups. Every time new interests appear, new groups may form on the basis of them. Groups come to crosscut one another in confusing abundance—indeed, in today's global society, there are so many groups and categories that nobody even tries to keep track of them all. Thus, with developed cultures, the complexity of the culture obscures the basic simplicity of the social structure. We cannot yet analyze any total culture because of that complexity. The Communist countries came a cropper on this point—their advance economic planning could not encompass all the factors in their culture.

SOCIAL STRUCTURES

Human beings are intensely social animals. The amount of time each of us spends with others is immense. But human beings are also highly creative in their sociality. When the size of any group increases, for example, new culture (including social culture) can be invented to keep the group from falling to pieces. History is full of examples: new types of leadership, based on roles with recognized authority, sprang up with the agricultural revolution of c. 5000 B.C. as people settled into larger communities, where kinship could no longer handle the load. Today, new kinds of social groups are emerging as global communications helps us to create worldwide interest groups.

There are three major forms found in any social structure:

1. the network,
2. the category,
3. the group.

A *social network* is made up of a number of linked dyads that contain no triads (See Figure 3–3). Linkages occur in the network because one person is involved with more than one other person, but the persons with whom he or she is involved are not directly involved with one another. Information can pass rapidly along networks. I have, several times in my life, been within three network dyads of the president of the United States. In one case, I know that my message got through, but I have never met that president or any other. If *A* is linked with *B* and is also linked to *C* and *D*, then information from *C* can readily reach *B* and *D* by virtue of their common relationship with *A*.

The network exists because dyads are chained, and hence many persons who do not know one another are nevertheless in touch with one another. As we shall see immediately below, if there are connecting links among members of the network, triads are introduced and social groups are thus formed.

Networking, as we shall see in the next chapter, is a social process in which people use the structure of the network. Human beings can use networks to specific social ends. But networks (a

FIGURE 3–3

A Social Network

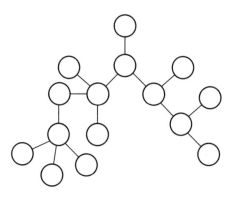

social form) may be present even when networking (a social process) is not a commonly used social principle.

Kinship systems or trading systems and international diplomatic systems are all networks. (The fact that groups may form within them will be considered below.) In current society, networking may be almost the only social process that keeps people connected to one another.

Social groups. Although it is sensible to argue that the dyad itself is a social group, more complex *social groups* are formed when three or more dyads are linked into a triad that acts as an entity (see Figure 3–4). When many groups exist in the same space, they must find ways to create ever larger and more complicated structures of relationship.

FIGURE 3–4

A Social Group as an Element of a Dyadic Relationship

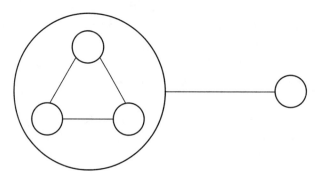

The individual members of a group may know each other, but they may not. A group is likely to have named positions or roles that its members occupy, and in terms of which they see and manipulate its structure—but it may not.

Categories are of a quite different order from networks and groups, but have to be considered carefully in this context because they are so commonly confused with groups. A *social category* is not based on dyads or triads or on relationships. Rather, it results from a cultural classification and evaluation of persons or groups on the basis of one or more of their characteristics. A social category is thus a schema—a cultural device for lumping persons together. Males and females are each a category. They do not necessarily form groups or networks (although gender may be used as a criterion for admission to some groups and many networks contain members of only one sex). What we call the human races are *social categories, culturally defined*. To believe them to be "racial" categories in some biological sense has created a lot of the havoc we live with. The old and the young may also be seen as culturally defined social categories.

These distinctions are extremely simple. However, if we confuse categories with groups, or either with networks, we can never understand the workings of the societies we live in.

SOCIALITY

Dyads, triads, networks, groups, and categories are the building blocks of society. We can now elucidate principles in accordance with which all social action, whether human or animal, is built. These principles resemble the axioms of geometry. They are the basis for creating and maintaining social structures; acts of using them fit together to become social processes. Variety among social groups stems from the fact that when the principles are culturized, the culturization can take many different forms. It is the varying culturization that provides the variety—and it also makes human groups seem more complex than in fact they are.

The number of principles that underlie sociality is small. I describe four of them in this chapter and seven in the next.[2]

Human beings share at least four—perhaps more—of the social principles with other animals: dominance, kinship, specialization of tasks, and cooperation. The other seven seem to me, at present, to be human inventions made possible by the use of culture, and will be considered in the next chapter. There are undoubtedly precursors of those other seven principles among nonhuman animals—it would be astonishing if there were not.

1. *Dominance.* The principle of dominance is widespread in the animal kingdom, underlying as it does all hierarchies. Dominance hierarchies derive from hormonally (and socially) triggered aggressive behavior. They are, in fact, one social device for keeping aggression from turning to conflict.

Americans and Europeans often confuse aggression with violence. In the process of applying the niceties that latter-day moralists have introduced, some people suggest that aggression is always unpleasant. It is not. Neither is it always associated with violence and bloodshed. Aggression arises from genetically encoded information, reinforced by experience and perhaps specialized by culture, that tells one when other animals are spatially too close for comfort. The criteria of "too close" are genetically encoded, but can be almost inexhaustibly refined by culture; these refinements are taught and learned.[3] Aggressive drives are involved with the hormone adrenalin, which triggers much of the energy we need to do whatever we have to do in order to survive and prosper. Without aggressive drives, we would perish.

All living animals must, to one degree or another, exhibit aggressive behavior—which is to say that they have to assert themselves to find a place in and resources from the environment. They may have to struggle with their neighbors to survive. Aggression, seen in this way, is one of the bases of evolution.

When people condemn aggression, they mean that they wish to change the cultural values that tell them which specific types of aggressive action to condemn and which to praise. They cannot actually get rid of aggression—their world would fall apart around them if they did. Most Americans teach their children that they should not start a fight, but they also teach them to stand up and fight if somebody else starts it. They tell them that aggressive competition in business is a good thing because it keeps prices down and deters businesses from fleecing the buying public.

The responses to aggression, in most animals, are

- to fight (destroy the other person);
- to flee (get out of the other person's orbit); or
- to settle for some position in a hierarchy (achieve a modus vivendi by admitting openly that some other persons outrank them).

Dominance is a factor associated with dyads: in an over-simple form, one party in a dyad is dominant, the other is submissive. When several such dyads are arranged together into a continuum (rather like a network), from the least powerful animal to the most powerful, we have a simple hierarchy of power.

Many animal species use the dominance hierarchy so that individuals can live together without having constantly either to fight each other or to flee, and so break their relationships and lose the advantages of sociality. Dominance hierarchies are not accompanied by high rates of conflict; rather, they reduce the need to turn aggressive behavior into conflict. Hierarchy works to maintain peace. The struggle is reduced to a series of gestures. Real fighting is found only when the hierarchy is being formed or when animals change their positions within it. We should not be surprised that, at the end of the Cold War, a string of conflicts erupted as various groups fought for position in the emerging new hierarchies.

A second mode of conflict reduction is territoriality, which is a device for isolating individuals or very small groups so that conflict is controlled. It is, of course, a social mechanism, but it limits relationships, so it cannot form the foundation of a more complex social system. Although territoriality will never vanish because it is so simple, it is nevertheless a very weak device for solving most social problems, as "isolationist" policies have repeatedly shown.

Culture can soften and alter the appearance of the modes of establishing and maintaining hierarchies, and has completely altered the context of territoriality. Hence hierarchy is more complicated among human beings than it is in most animal societies; human beings see territoriality as a matter of legal rights and ownership—at least they do in cultural systems in which the market principle is central. Human beings can also hide raw hierarchy when the principle of dominance is combined with other social principles, particularly the principle of role (which is described in the next chapter), to create governments and bureaucracies.

2. *Kinship*. Kinship concerns reproduction, and therefore shared genes as well as sexuality. Most birds and (at least, female) mammals recognize their own young. Their parenting behavior consists in nest-building, hatching, feeding the young, and protecting them against predators and against each other. Such behavior is the basis of kinship.

A second dimension of the principle of kinship has, of course, to do with sexuality.[4] Sexual behavior is genetically coded behavior, but human beings have overlaid their innate sexuality with cultural taboos and requirements, and with psychological rewards and uncertainties, to the point where there is little left about it that can be considered merely "natural."

Because human beings, like other mammals, must be nursed for the earliest period of their lives, they spend that time in intense social relationships with their mothers. Fathers are more peripheral among many species, but among many bird species both sexes do the parenting; among some mammals, the male carries on at least some parenting activities. And the invention of the nursing bottle has, among some human societies, thrust men into new parenting activities.

Psychoanalysts use the term *libido* to include both sexual appetite and the urge to parent the young. It is a combination of the urges, including the cultural urges, that can be called life-protecting or life-enhancing.

Human kinship systems are cultural extensions and refinements of the basic recognitions that arise from parenting and sexuality—the principles of sexual reproduction. Those systems are made up of biological kin plus other people who have opted to treat one another as kin.[5] The cultural changes that can be rung on the biological facts and the cultural extension of them are myriad, but they can be (and, by and large, have been) discerned as patterns by anthropologists.

The culturization of kinship has provided what appears to be an immense variety in the structures and rules of the human family. That variety stems from the many facts that the culturization can emphasize and from the many modes of successful reproduction. If one focuses on the variety, the basic simplicity and similarity of all human reproduction can be missed.

3.   *Specialization of Tasks.* The social principle of specialization is found in most vertebrate species, including all mammals. For most of them it is a simple differentiation by sex: adult males perform different social tasks from adult females. However, among human beings, the division of tasks into men's work or women's work becomes ever increasingly a cultural arrangement. Given highly efficient culture, a new context has emerged: except for the specialized male and female functions in reproduction, there is no men's work that cannot be done by women and no women's work that cannot be done by men, in spite of the fact that gender remains an important determinant of who does what. In general, the more technical culture is available, the easier it is to erase the gender barrier in the division of labor.[6]

In most animal societies, male and female each have their biologically given tasks. The fact that each performs them with a reasonable degree of dependability is part of the cement of their society. But the two genders are also likely to be seeking different ends. Therefore, cooperation—even communication—between the two may sometimes be a little chancy.

The limitations on human females created by their reproductive burden began to be eroded when the nursing bottle was invented in France early in the last century. It was further eroded when human females became able to separate their sex lives from their reproductive lives by use of contraceptives. Some human males in many societies today approach reproduction in much the same way that females are said to approach it: putting a lot of energy into rearing the young that are already born rather than (or at least in addition to) merely spreading their genes as widely as possible.

Age is also a basis for division of social tasks. Young animals, including people, do different jobs than do their elders.

Human beings have, using culture, added many new modes of dividing tasks. Indeed, the more complex the society becomes, the greater the need for division and the more specialized the criteria for division are likely to be. People can specialize by aptitude (an efficient mode with minimal waste of talent, although it may put a heavy load of choice on individual persons). They can be assigned tasks because their parents were who they were—a way to do it that is extremely wasteful of talent. The various jobs are all needed to keep the society afloat; every smoothly functioning society has a reward system that leads individuals to do what is expected of them.

4. *Cooperation.* In biology, *cooperation* is a general term meaning activities for the common benefit of organisms living together. Although this kind of simple cooperation can be observed in the nonhuman world, explaining it in terms of Darwinian fitness theory remained difficult as long as the basic assumption was the individual's struggle for existence. Why should any organism help another organism to survive if it was also competing with that other organism for food and for reproduction? Our views on the matter changed in the 1970s when sociobiologists became aware of the gene's-eye view, which sees the organism as merely the host that is needed to create a never-ending string of copies of its genes. In the process, they discovered that organisms often behave altruistically if the altruist shares genes with the beneficiary. In this view, one organism helps another to survive if that organism has many of the same genes, and those could be propagated better by the beneficiary than by the altruist. Kinship, in other words, is the cradle of cooperation.

Among human beings, culturized cooperation follows the same general rule: a number of people working together toward a cultural goal can often reach that goal where individuals cannot do it alone. However, new issues—cultural issues—have been added that may prove difficult in some contexts. Cooperation can be turned into a moral virtue regardless of its context or its outcome—and that may be dangerous. Further, there may be a regrettable tendency to lump cooperation with harmony, which is something quite different.[7] Thus, turning cooperation into a virtue instead of using it when it is profitable for survival can turn out to be a real cultural trap.

Yet another variable in cooperation is the time dimension.[8] If two individuals of the same species meet only once, it is in the interest of each *not* to cooperate with the other. But if they meet habitually, then both can benefit if they help each other.

The question thereupon becomes, under what social conditions is cooperation more rewarding than exploitation? It is, in fact, the recurring question in every long-term relationship, including parenthood. Am I giving more than I am getting? Am I willing to continue to do that?

Cooperation with strangers is rarely found in the nonhuman world. Indeed, it would not be very sensible, because the creature who refuses to cooperate and insists on taking all the benefit for himself always wins. If A *always* cooperates, B can cheat him. Therefore, the principle of cooperation needs rules to stop the cheating. The most obvious of these rules derive from the kinship principle. The principle of cooperation found among creatures sharing the same genes can be extended, by people, to those sharing the same culture and values, paying homage to the same gods, or being ruled by the same chieftains. But the boundary of cooperation and exploitation has to be worked out carefully in each situation. Who will cheat?

For cooperation to be completely effective, no individual can be allowed to get away with cheating. Those who are cheated can retaliate. The cooperating individuals must each have something at stake: if I cheat you and win, I nevertheless lose on some other front. Hierarchy is often the basis of human social arrangements to control cheating, especially within communities.

The cooperation of kin is still the surest form of cooperation among human beings, as among all creatures. An old Tiv told me around 1950 that the surest way to get loyal followers was to beget them. But community can also create the assurance of cooperation. In a small community, everybody will still be there tomorrow, so that people cooperate rather than risk social ostracism. No matter how much they may hate one another, they will cooperate in most matters because the rewards of cooperation are greater than the reward of noncooperation minus the punishment for noncooperation. Said in symbols:

$$RC > RnonC - P$$

People can, in some circumstances, win more by cheating than by cooperating. But if the punishment for cheating is well designed, they also lose more if they cheat. Indeed, they can, if their kin or community turn on them, lose everything.

The rest of the social principles are, as far as I know, limited to human societies and will be discussed in the next chapter. Here the point is that culture—tools and meanings—has turned kinship into families and family values as well as descent groups and other types of social group; hierarchy has become bureaucracy and order. Specialization of tasks has been turned by culture into professions and into gender struggles; culture has turned cooperation into virtue—indeed, whole philosophical systems, religions, political policies, and economic attitudes can be based on *culturized* cooperation.

Chapter 4

What Culture Does to Society II

Human Social Organization

The study of human development reveals a difficulty that is meaningful for our study of social principles. When physical growth is completed, at the end of adolescence, developmental psychologists and psychiatrists must suddenly change how they view their patients—they have to find a new criterion with which to gauge continuing development. We have been traditionally taught that development means growth, and that growth has to do with increase in size and development of our physical capacities, specifically sexuality. Hence the (false) idea that when we have reached our full size, our "growth" is over.

Neither development nor aging ends with mere physical maturity. When we have to abandon physical growth as the guiding variable, uncertainty sets in. Thus, psychological development in adulthood has been poorly studied in our culture or anywhere else, in part because it is difficult for us to measure. We have no agreed place to start, no accepted basic premise for that stage of the life course.

Just so, in the study of the principles of social organization, we are on firm ground when we examine the culturization of behavior that is built into the human animal. The animal underpinning remains clear even while it is elaborated into full human status by

37

culturization. But a certain professional insecurity sets in when we have to abandon animal behavior as our index.[1]

Cultured creatures do indeed create new principles of social organization that are more than mere culturizations of animal behavior. These new social principles derive from cultural processes themselves. These new rules cannot successfully gainsay or contradict the animal nature of the human creature (though they often try), but they cannot exist at all outside of human culture. In the absence of biological measures, where can we find direction?

A second difficulty emerges. Differing cultural ways can provide adequate solutions to the same problem. And because new cultural ways can develop rapidly, new cultural manifestations may emerge suddenly even if there is little change in the underlying pattern. Such manifestations complicate the processes of observation. The study of animal behavior—like ethnography—begins with observation. But the premises underlying observation of nonhuman animals can be readily stated; observers can be fairly readily trained so that their observations will be comparable. No doubt there are differences in the animal observations of scientists who were brought up and trained in different cultures; certainly there are differences in the problems they select. Yet those differences become insignificant when compared to the difficulties of cultural bias on the part of observers of human beings.

Cultural observation can be made only by observers who are themselves already enculturated. Such observers need to correct for their own culture (including training) as they observe other cultures. Doing so requires an unusual capacity to see one's own culture as an *attribute* of one's self rather than as part of the *essence* either of one's self or of the natural world. Many students (and, indeed, some respected professionals) can parrot that remark better than they can actually apply it. All of us have blind spots; and working out such blind spots is the constant struggle of the cultural anthropologist.

It is a common contention that every scholar's observations must be accompanied by as full an analysis as possible of the observers' training and biases. Otherwise, observations may vary so widely that they cannot be compared with any degree of security. Worse, different scholars may not even be able to recognize whether or not they are even talking about the same thing.

To make a comparison with an example from outside social science: the study of the human genome (a catalogue of all of the genes found in our species) focuses on observations that scientists from different cultures can fairly readily come to agree are "facts." However, when we examine cultural matters, the difficulty of defining the problem may be all but insurmountable— specifically because the observers cannot agree on precisely what they are observing. When we study other human beings, the answers to the questions are implied by the questions in a way that is not true to the same degree in biology or physics. For just such reasons, we shall probably never get a list of social principles or cultural categories that everybody can agree on. Fortunately, this problem can be made irrelevant if we all understand that it is there.

There are thus two major problems in studying culture-dependent social principles:

- the cultural stance of the observer, and
- the protean character of the cultural traditions being observed.

The following are some more of the principles that I have managed to isolate. My first four principles are set forth in the previous chapter. They may not be the same ones that other investigators would isolate. We should understand that this particular kind of diversity is a *strength* of social science, not a weakness.

5. *Contact*. Contract came into prominence in social science when jurist Henry Sumner Maine discovered, in his researches published as *Ancient Law* in 1861,[3] that the history of law moves from a law of status (that is, kinship and locality) to a law of contract. *Contract* is quite different from *cooperation* in that it implies not just reciprocity, and not just working together to complete a task. A contract is, rather, an overt agreement in which two parties (either individuals or groups) agree that they will exchange specific, named, identifiable goods or services. One party will provide one named thing in return for something complementary to be

supplied by the other. The relationship between shark and pilot fish, or that between African cattle and the cattle egret, undoubtedly provides reciprocal benefits; they may be based on a sort of reciprocity, but they are not contract. We must take care when we draw the lines among reciprocity, the precursors of contract, contract itself, and metaphors of contract.

Today, given the rise of ethology and other advances in biology, we can see something that Maine could not have seen: that the principle of contract is one effective way of dealing with relationships with strangers. Small-scale human societies are not plagued by strangers—indeed, in such societies strangers are immediately suspect and are likely to be instantly classed as enemies. But as societies become larger and as their cultures grow more complex, the number of strangers increases. With that increase comes the need for a system to deal predictably with strangers. More or less formalized contract is one way to achieve that predictability.

For contracts to be predictable and trusted, a society must develop a legal system with the capacity and the willingness to enforce agreements and apply sanctions. With such a system in place, the ultimate measures for enforcement can be and generally are taken out of the hands of the parties to the agreement. This means that the conditions of the contract have to be spelled out in detail—in far greater detail than is ever necessary for agreements between kinsmen or long-term neighbors. In the process of spelling out the details, certain aspects of culture become rigidified. The larger a human society gets, and the more complex its culture becomes, the more likely it is that its realm of overtly rigidified rules will expand—and contract with it.

An important point is contained in these examples: as societies get larger, and cultures more complex, it is no longer possible for everybody to deal with everything. Specialists emerge. With them come specialized institutions that take over some tasks from the more general institutions—especially from the family, kinship groups, and locality. German sociologist Georg Simmel pointed out a century ago that such social differentiation means that new culture arises to keep the various specialist institutions communicating and working together.

In small towns, business can be handled by a handshake or a nod and verbal agreement—everyone in town knows everyone else, and anybody who isn't "as good as his word" is exposed, shunned, and ultimately ostracized. But once such a group grows beyond the size at which everybody can know everybody else and can trust or distrust others because their characters are known to all—and because the kinship system has built-in sanctions that need not be specified—the culture has to become more complex, and some of it has to be made more explicit and more rigid. Such complexity, the increased number of strangers, and the increased rigidity set the stage for contract.

Complex legal systems that rigidify cultural expectation in the service of dealing with strangers are part of a specialized political hierarchy. A legal system, as part of a specialized political system, can and will provide sanctions against failure to fulfill contracts. Lack of repeated interaction has just as important a part to play in contract as it does in cooperation.

6.   *Role.* One of the most astonishing changes in human pre-history occurred when people began to differentiate between a role and the person who fills the role. This differentiation lies at the basis of the state form of government, starting with king-ship—"The king is dead, long live the king!"—and the require-ments of orderly succession. It is evident in all political or religious offices. It is the soul of bureaucracy. A bureaucracy is a hierarchy of roles or offices, thus involving at least two social prin-ciples.

7.   *Ranking.* Ranking is evaluating things on a scale from most desirable to least desirable. People can and do rank roles. They rank individual people, ideas, categories, and items of material culture. By ranking things conceptually, they are doing something different from creating a simple hierarchy. Ideas must be distinguished from their ranking in precisely the same way that role-players must be distinguished from roles. As a result of this kind of ranking, kings (a category) are said to be "better" than commoners (another category in the same schema). People rank positions (roles) in culturally complex organizations of pro-duction so that managers rank above workers; they rank culture traits (both possessions and modes of behaving) so that a fine porcelain dinner service confers more prestige than crockery does, or using one vocabulary indicates higher rank than using

another. People rank jobs, clothing, whatever. Lloyd Warner found in Yankee City (a made-up name for Newburyport, Massachusetts) in the 1930s and 1940s that its residents even ranked the magazines they displayed on their coffee tables. People are likely, then, to create categories on the basis of their distinctions, and give the categories force by using social pressures to maintain or change the rankings.

It seems to be the case in our Western culture at the present time that the distribution of powers, roles, and ranking is undergoing profound change as the force of the information revolution erupts around us. Too complex a hierarchy would seem to be incompatible with the free movement of information; the content of roles is opening up to the awareness of all; rankings are more open and examinable. Blue sky is appearing everywhere.

8. *Property*. Recognizing property in goods may be the basis of a lot of relationships between people, but because we do not have a *social* relationship with the goods we own (dogs or other pets may constitute a sort of exception), property is not itself a social principle. Rather, ideas and rules about property may be manifest in the operation of several social principles. However, if one person can hold property rights in other people (as against kinship rights or citizenship rights), a special principle *is* required. To sell one's labor on the market is a matter of contract. You may say that you are the slave of your employer, but that is only a metaphor—although the cost might be impossibly high, legally you *can* quit your job. In spite of the fact that the boss may sometimes behave as if he or she owns you, you are *not* the boss's property. You may sometimes feel that you have been forced, totally against your will, into a nonkinship, noncontract relationship in which you have lost all or a significant part of what people today call your human rights. But such a feeling does not literally make you the legal property of the boss or the company.

Almost all civilizations have, in their history, passed through a period of slavery. Slavery is not just a form of labor allocation; it also involves the way outsiders can be brought into a society. What do you do with captives? Male captives were sacrificed in some societies, and female captives were sometimes married, sometimes taken as concubines or turned into prostitutes. Strangers, both

males and females, can be turned into slaves and made to produce agricultural goods or other wealth.

9. *The Market Principle.* In analyzing the behavior of many
animal species, scholars have discussed the cost–benefit aspects of
the relationships among the individual animals. Their point is
that when many animals make choices independently, as many
do, more or less unintended social results may occur. When we
apply the same kind of analysis to human beings, we realize that
demography, for example, is the result of individual decisions
about health practices, reproductive practices, and marriage
practices. The impact of divorce rates on the family system of the
society, or individual decisions to drink alcohol or not to drink it,
are examples of multiple individual decisions with broad social
fallout. In all these cases, the individual decision and the unintended social results are not consciously linked by the behaving
creature, animal or human. Nobody ever stayed married just to
reduce the overall divorce rate.

However, some human societies have turned cost–benefit into
an overt principle of social organization. "The market" is a prime
example. The market principle is a mechanism that ably provides
for the distribution of goods. Yet, from the standpoint of human
suffering, the uncontrolled market may also be the source of
many difficulties.[4] The social cost of substituting other principles
of distributing goods in the interest of reducing people's suffering
(e.g., putting a government bureaucracy in charge of production
and distribution decisions) would seem, in large-scale society, to
be very high. Even trying to separate the inequities of the society
into parts (the economic sector, the welfare sector) is costly. The
problem is how a society can reap the broad economic benefit of
the market while reducing its costs to individuals.

Tastes in food lead to social results in accordance with the market principle. In the years after 1965, Americans individually
changed their diets in response to fuller scientific information.
They have done it several times since. The impact on business has
been immense. When it was discovered in the late 1980s that oat
bran can be instrumental in lowering blood cholesterol if one
adheres to a low-fat, low-calorie diet, some unknown but huge
portion of the population began to eat oat bran. The Quaker Oats

Company had a field day; other American traders began to import oats from Australia. When it was subsequently discovered that eating oat bran without *also* eating less fat and calories doesn't much affect cholesterol levels, a lot of Americans gave up oat bran. Obviously, individual decisions have great impact on social (including economic) situations.

Although the market mechanism may be found in many societies—that is, price as a mediation between supply and demand—a society must be of a certain large scale before the invisible and unintended effects of the cost–benefit principle become crucial. When they are present in smaller-scale societies, the results seem to go unnoticed. The discipline of economics, which specializes in studying supply and demand, came into existence in the late 1700s, just when it was needed. People before the French physiocrats or Adam Smith already behaved more or less in accordance with what were to become economic principles—but then, so do many nonhuman animals. The discipline, however, was new.

10. *Networking*. We saw in the last chapter that the network is one of the basic social forms. Each of us can be enmeshed in many networks, whose membership may overlap only in ourselves. However, consciously using the network as a principle of social process in situations when organizations based on other social principles have proved inadequate is fairly new. Networks became an anthropological concern in the 1950s, but the word *network* became a verb only in the 1970s.

If you want a new job, you network. That is, you put out the word among your friends, acquaintances, kin and colleagues, who then put out the word among *their* kin, colleagues, and acquaintances. The strength of, and the degree of reciprocity in, the dyads of the network determine the avidity with which all will keep you in mind. Networking works in the modern world, but is scarcely known in small-scale societies where the social system is dominated by kinship or one of the other principles, and where the overwhelming number of relationships are face to face.

11. *Mass Audience Manipulation and Public Relations*. My final social principle came into being only with the invention of printing. Although audiences existed long before the printing press, those audiences were face-to-face audiences. Storytellers and

dramatists did indeed have audiences. Philosophers like Plato understood the importance of the audience. Before printing, however, there could be no mass audience; that had to wait for mass literacy.

Mass audiences were slow to form. Something called the reading public began to be a mass audience, and it became powerful. But its real power began to show itself only in this century, with the invention and general availability of radio. And the mass audience became even more powerful with the advent and wide spread of television in the 1950s. The use of the mass audience as a specific social tool, like the use of the network, is a product of large-scale society and the vast explosion of cultural information.

The place of public relations—of getting a message either to a mass audience or to some specifically defined segment of it—has grown as this social principle has expanded.

New examples of these seven human ways to behave together come up constantly. New modes of communication like Project Iridium (which proposes an elaborate satellite system to link cellular telephones throughout the world), or the Infonet and Internet, which will ultimately allow all the information in the world (including, of course, all the nonsense and disinformation) to be recoverable from a simple desktop computer are now altering social structures and will almost surely lead to new social principles. New, faster, more convenient transportation techniques will bring us more strangers and more novelty, as well. Although the cultural medium of social relations may change, the human act of turning society into a tool, then finding new ways to use it, is one of the most important innovations in human history; it is capable of almost infinite cultural complexification, and hence of almost infinite adaptability.

Part II

Cultural Dynamics[1]

Culture is a set of common understandings, manifest in act and artifact.[2]
*It is in two places at once: inside somebody's head as understandings and
in the external environment as act and artifact. If it isn't truly present in
both spheres, it is only incomplete culture. Psychotherapists deal mainly
with the understandings, which puts them at a disadvantage in getting at
what they call "reality." Archaeologists work almost entirely with the artifacts, which puts them at a disadvantage in dealing with people's ideas.*

*If you think of culture as a subject noun, then it has to do something or
undergo something if it is to change. In that context, the dynamics are easy
to ignore. But if you see culture as a predicate, it* is *change. It encompasses
its own capacity for change—it is a sort of hydra, made up of many combined individual human actions and reactions.*

Chapter 5

Chains

Trajectories and Cycles

It is as important to know how culture works as it is to know how the universe works or how the body works. Culture is a vast data bank, but it also provides the program for controlling and using the data. Therefore we must first begin by separating the process from the data.

Action chains[1] are the essential basis of culture dynamics. Actions and events follow one another in predictable chains, sometimes founded on cause and effect, sometimes only on cultural tradition. Unless it is disturbed a known sequence of acts, once begun, is usually followed through. Although the participants have the option of removing themselves from most action chains, the price may be very high. Moreover, only with the completion of the sequence can any of the actions do what the actors intended them to do. The same actions, in different contexts outside the sequence, may well have utterly different meanings and effects. Correct sequence imparts meaning and efficiency to action chains.

We all know that there is a "right" way to do things (and then, as the saying goes, there's the army way). The "rightness" may be physical and material or it may be cultural, marked by criteria of appropriateness or efficiency. Carpentry is a case in point—you can't put a roof on a house before the supports are in place. If the required actions are not followed in the right order, the resulting structure will probably collapse—if, indeed, it can be built at all. There are also sequential differences in cooking that lead to different results, even when the ingredients are the same. An African groundnut stew contains chicken, peanuts, and pepper (and may contain onions and okra). Chinese Gum Pao Chicken contains chicken, peanuts, and pepper. You would never believe from the taste that the major differences are not so much in the African optional additives as in the order and speed of cooking.

A predictable sequence of actions or events is as important in social life as in cooking; it is also just as important as the ingredients, be they values or laws or religion.

ACTION CHAINS: INDIVIDUAL AND SOCIAL

Some chains are series of actions that can be performed by a single individual, but two-person action chains are far more common. In the most common form, the act of one person is followed by a predictable act of the second—and so on until a mutually recognized goal is reached.

A two-person chain implies two feedback mechanisms of the sort that were described in Chapter 2. Each person is in the perceptual space of the other; they cannot help being affected by one another. To examine two-person chains requires looking at the nature of a social relationship, in light of what was said in Chapter 2 about the human being as a feedback device.

Under conditions in which predictable repeated actions occur, common understandings emerge (the "collective representations" of French sociology). Such common understandings form the basis of *a culture* (which is quite different from *culture*-without-an-article). Their common culture must be inside both actors, even though it can probably never be made identical in the two. It is also outside them, "manifest in act and artifact." The standard for the results to be achieved becomes something with which each of them must struggle and compromise. That standard affects the relationship and affects the acts performed by each person, which in turn affect the standard. That standard is, thus, one of the building blocks of cultures with an -s—the plural of *culture-with-an-article*.[2]

Expressed another way, for the interaction of two or more people to be successful, all parties must be able to predict the outcome. Such predictability demands not only that the actions of each proceed in a specific order, but that all of the sets of actions be interlinked. Edward T. Hall[3] has described the action chain as a dance and has noted that the common goal could be reached only after each link in the chain was forged.

Interlinking two sets of actions—one from each of the two participants—leads to a sort of unitary feedback device, held in place by the two participants. The dynamic processes in the relationship so formed take on a life of their own, not totally determined by either actor, as both react to the environment that includes the other. Their interaction is a beast with two heads, to paraphrase both Shakespeare and Villon.

Hall gave, as a simple example of an action chain, the fifteen ordered steps required in the mating of sticklebacks. He then argues that human beings do *nothing* that is not part of an action chain—a powerful statement.[4] As we have noted, nonsocial action chains occur in the behavior of single individuals—a cook, working alone in the kitchen, for example. However, all social behavior comprises action chains. Games like checkers or bridge proceed along action chains, as does solitaire. Courtship is an action chain. Brushing your teeth is an action chain.

At every action in the chain, each participant has the option of leaving the field—not completing the next action, and so disrupting the chain. This does not mean that all behavior is not part of some action chain. To opt out of one chain is to enter another.

The very fact that two such persons working together affect one another means that the external standard must be made clear and explicit so that the internal standards are reassuring to each. The internal and external standards can be made to converge so that dissonance between the understandings of the two persons will be reduced. The internal standard that results in the person is the product of experience and can be called a *character structure*. The external standard is the product of the interaction and performance; it can be called *a culture* (the article is important).

FIGURE 5–1

Two Individuals Interacting Form a Dyad, the Basic Social Unit

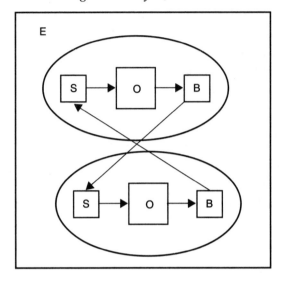

The situation of the dyad is represented in Figure 5–1. It can be read: a social dyad (S–B) exists when each of two persons is part of the environment (E) to which the other is reacting. When time and expectations (O) are added, action chains are formed.

ACTION CHAINS AND EVENT CHAINS

The earliest successful exploration of action chains is to be found in Arnold van Gennep's 1908 book *Les Rites de Passage*. It is summarized briefly in Figure 5–2, which can be read: a person is first ritually removed from his or her social position, then is withdrawn into a threshold position or state.[5] The person, while in the threshold state, is subjected to rituals that are designed to transform him or her, after which the person is brought back into real society in a new set of roles. Van Gennep outlined this process in the context of studying formal rites of passage, but it applies very broadly.

Van Gennep discovered that this stripped-down event chain was widespread among the world's societies. I would go so far as to say that when recognition of rites of passage is not present, one of the major simplifying social devices is missing—people who live

FIGURE 5–2

Event Chain: Rites of Passage

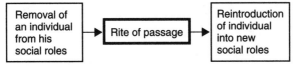

without rites of passage find growing up and changing roles more personally complicated that do people who use them. On the other hand, in times that Robert Jay Lifton calls the era of "Protean Man," the absence of rites of passage may keep our identities loose and so facilitate a capacity for constant and rapid adjustment to changed environment conditions.[6] In either case, as we shall see in the next chapter, the absence of structured rites of passage does not mean an absence of either threshold states or action chains.

Building on van Gennep's insights, in 1957 Victor Turner and I independently examined event chains in terms of an African legal system, though neither of us used the term. The behavior of the Tiv whom I studied allowed me to separate the legal from ritual far more than did (or could) the Ndembu allow it of Turner, but that point is not important to the present one. The event chain[7] for describing a legal system is set out in Figure 5–3(a). Turner's chain, which he called *social drama*, and which I have turned into a flowchart is shown in Figure 5–3(b).[8] Turner's added step—escalating the breach of a crisis before the next phase occurs—fit his Ndembu data clearly. My Tiv data do not require that step, but certainly do not contradict it. The point is that all event chains can be broken into smaller, more detailed, more specific event chains.

More important than specific variations in the model event chain is the prior realization that *all* behavior forms chains. Chains are everywhere, and they promise the best means for comparing cultures—certainly far better than culture traits or clusters. All too often, however, anthropologists fail to note chains in the first place. Consider, for example, variations in household: Meyer Fortes once turned what had previously been seen as a typology of households into an event chain, finding that what

FIGURE 5–3

Event Chains of Legal Action

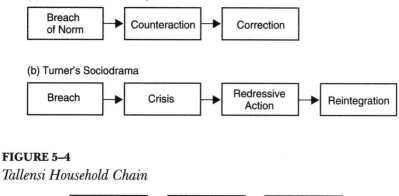

(a) Bohannan's Event Sequence

(b) Turner's Sociodrama

FIGURE 5–4

Tallensi Household Chain

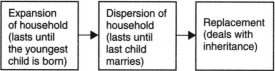

appeared to be "types" of households among the Tallensi are, when seen through time, phases in a long-term chain in which households first grow by accretion and expansion, then shrink as more and more people move out. My reconstruction of his analysis of Tallensi households, expressed as an event chain, is set forth in Figure 5–4.

The work that followed on Fortes's insight is, as far as I know, unfortunately all dedicated to finding other societies in which household classifications can be so explained rather than developing the more inclusive question of action chains.

An event chain can bog down, making satisfactory closure impossible. The feud is an example. A feud is a chain of legal action that has struck a cultural trap and cannot be brought to completion because the people involved cannot discern any honorable means of escape from the trap. In Figure 5–5, one party performs an act, say a killing. The relatives of the victim apply the counteraction of another killing. However, the counteraction is not interpreted as such by the original killers, who brand it a further breach of norm. Cultures that put up with feuds—and per-

FIGURE 5–5

The Incomplete Event Chain of the Feud

haps most other cultures as well—lack adequate face-saving devices.

TRAJECTORIES AND CYCLES

Chains can be classified into two types. The first, which we have already examined, exhibits an easily definable beginning, middle, and end. It can be called a trajectory. But other chains fold back on themselves, thus creating cycles.

The event chain associated with marriage is a cycle, and it is much the same in all societies. As is evident in Figure 5–6, marriages begin with an arrangement or a courtship that culminates in a wedding. Weddings may differ so much in their externals as to be almost unrecognizable cross-culturally, but they always fit into this kind of chain. After the wedding, a marital relationship is either established or formalized; its content also shows vast cultural variation. All marriages end, either at the death of one of the spouses or at the time of some action, comparable to our idea of divorce, that dissolves the marriage while both parties (and whoever of their kinsmen are intimately involved) continue to live. After the dissolution, a period of widowhood occurs for the surviving partner or partners. The state of widowhood is usually treated very differently from the various states of divorce. In societies that allow remarriage, this event chain forms a cycle—the widowed survivor can marry again, starting through a new version of the chain. In societies that allow polygamy, several such chains may be going at once.

Both cycles and trajectories may be repeated any number of times in different instances. The fact that a trajectory does not fold back on itself does not mean that you or somebody else cannot do it repeatedly. It means only that each time you go through it, the chain completes itself rather than taking you back to

FIGURE 5–6

The Event Chain of a Marriage

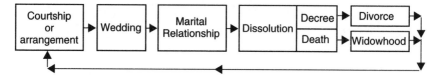

Square One (or anywhere else in the chain). Cycles may never reach closure—what can be seen in one sense as completion may also be seen as merely arriving yet again at the point from which another lap can begin.

TRANSACTIONAL CHAINS AND CAREER CHAINS

Another way to classify action chains is to distinguish *transactions* from *careers*. Transaction chains refer to acts in a relationship between two parties concerning their interests or rights in a thing. Career chains focus on persons. Although John Dewey said it, and Hohfeld said it, and many other scholars have said it, I wish to start from Michael Thompson's statement[9] of the distinction:

• *Transactional chains* are initiated by the introduction of a particular object into the system and terminated by its removal. Such chains focus on the histories of objects. The basic question is: how are objects socially processed? An automobile is manufactured, then sold to its original buyer, who trades it in after two years, whereupon it is bought by a widow just returning to work after her bereavement. She keeps it for eleven years, and would sell it for junk except that the man who buys it knows there is a market for it if he can turn it into an antique. The automobile had been, through many transactions, socially processed pretty thoroughly.

• *Career chains* focus on people or social groups and therefore concern the careers of persons or the histories of social groups. The basic question is: how are human beings and organizations born; how do they grow, wither, and die?

Careers are trajectories initiated by the entry of a particular person into social life and terminated by that person's exit from social life. Developmental psychology and psychiatry have provided a number of models for growing up and growing old in our own society, but cross-cultural studies of such physical and psychological development are in their infancy. Management science has begun to look at what might be called the "life course" of organizations, but this field is also in its infancy.

Transaction chains are built around a string of relationships each surrounding the same object. Frederik Barth[10] limited the word *transaction* to "those sequences of interaction which are systematically governed by reciprocity." I would expand the notion to utilize principles beyond reciprocity—to redistributional as well as market methods of distributing objects. But Barth realizes that not just economic value, but every other kind of value (thus, moral "values"), derives from chains made up of transactions. A transaction chain can be analyzed in terms of the strategies of game theory—that is, the motivations of the participants at every transactions can be analyzed, and their strategies in the transactions computed. Each of those transactions is a dyadic interaction—and, of course, game theory assumes the primacy of the dyad.

RUBBISH THEORY

Game theory has been developed to a sophisticated degree by mathematically inclined social scientists. But it is not the only "game" in town. Michael Thompson extended Barth's concerns by introducing an idea he called "rubbish theory." His immediate concern was with the objects or ideas that people do *not* take into the next link of the chain: with things they throw away, either by discarding them or by denying their relevance or even their existence, and excluding them from their actions, even their thinking. The discarded or denied "rubbish" may stay, more or less hidden, somewhere in the system. When anything that has been thrown away reappears to haunt and throw off that system, he calls it an "excluded monster." Thompson's step was an important one directly into cultural process theory.

Thompson recognized that all material items and some ideas can be ranked along a trajectory in which an object proceeds from (1) transience through (2) a rubbish phase to become (3) a durable object (see Figure 5–7). Antiques (his example is a Queen Anne tallboy) have durable value—they are objects or ideas that

FIGURE 5–7

The Premises Underlying Thompson's Rubbish Theory

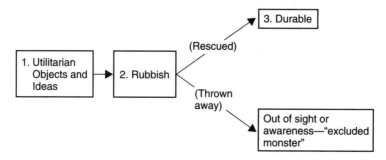

might once have been rubbish but have been rescued from that category. A used car is transient—it will soon be rubbish. But a few used cars are resurrected from the rubbish category. With a combination of good luck, loving care, and a market created by collectors, they are turned into classic cars.

The rubbish category, which is situation between transient and utilitarian objects on one side and durable treasures on the other, is a "region of flexibility" that works just like the threshold state in a rite of passage. Within that flexible region, our actions with regard to objects determine our view of them. A thing or idea in that rubbish category may be either thrown away, perhaps destroyed, or may become an excluded monster—but it may also be rescued into the durable category.

Thompson illustrates this kind of event chain with the history of textilographs called Stevensgraphs, which were cheap loom-woven pictures that were made before the eyes of, and sold for about a shilling each to, the people who came to marvel at the York (England) Exhibition of 1879. These woven pictures were turned out by the hundreds of thousands for working-class Victorian sitting rooms. Then, with the changes of taste that came with the first third of the twentieth century, Stevensgraphs became rubbish. Most were thrown away. But a few were spared, and one of those shilling textilographs sold at an art auction in 1971 for £75. The question is: how did a bit of rubbish become a treasure and achieve increasing value?

Thompson asked the same question about housing. A house has a limited life expectancy. In modern cities, at least, some houses go through a rubbish phase, in slums. Most slum houses are ultimately torn down. However, a few are restored and may even become historic landmarks. The other important premise is that *all* rubbish is either destroyed—which means reduced to forms that are no longer recognizable by processes such as burning or grinding or weathering, thus staying in the system in only a derivative form—or else it remains an integral part of the system. There is no "away" into which anything can be thrown. To paraphrase Gertrude Stein, there is no away away. Social scientists (and everybody else) must live with their insight that everything is, and remains, connected.

To take another example from a different part of the world, the Tiv of Nigeria have a category of ancestors that can be called rubbish ancestors (though they would not recognize or appreciate this characterization)—a category that helps them to keep the balance between their ancestral genealogies and their this-world political organization as it changes over time. There is, in the top reaches of their genealogies, a durable category of ancestors from ancient times—some twelve generations or so. Then a transient category is made up of the ancestors that living people remember—perhaps four, at most five generations. However, between the durable ancestors and the transient-recent ancestors is a "rubbish" category of ancestors. As time goes on, and old memories are replaced by younger ones, the older transient-recent ancestors pass into this rubbish category. All the "rubbish" ancestors who are not needed to keep the genealogies and the actual political realities aligned disappear from memory; most rubbish ancestors ultimately leave no trace. A few of them, however, may be made durable when the living and changing social organization requires the presence of another node in the lineage genealogy. This process has allowed the genealogies to remain consonant with the social facts on the ground.[11]

Ideas work much like the textilographs, the slum houses, or "rubbish" ancestors. Thompson notes that if (by definition or any other way) we exclude ideas from our theorizing, those ideas behave like rubbish. Such "excluded monsters" may come back to haunt the system. The idea that a scientist's personal "subjective" perceptions can be ruled out of scientific experiments and considerations creates this kind of excluded monster. The excluded

FIGURE 5–8

Some Types of Action Chain

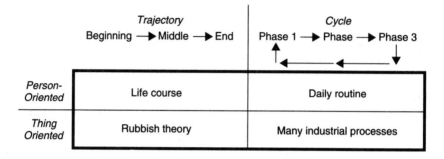

	Trajectory Beginning → Middle → End	Cycle Phase 1 → Phase → Phase 3
Person-Oriented	Life course	Daily routine
Thing Oriented	Rubbish theory	Many industrial processes

ideas can be denied, only to sneak unbidden back into our lives and thoughts. Ideas have to be either disproved or else dealt with.

The various types of action chains that we have distinguished are summarized in Figure 5–8.

Action chains are a means of getting at the simplest facts of cultural dynamics. Examining them is far more fruitful in cross-cultural studies than examining either single cultural traits or collections of traits. Some chains are trajectories; some are cycles. But, one way or another, everything we do can be seen in terms of action chains. The chain is at the basis of the dynamics of culture and society—and hence at the foundation of any study of the dynamics of culture.

Chapter 6

Transformation and Recontexting

A culture that cannot change is a dead culture. Innovation is a vital part of cultural dynamics.

Cultural change occurs whenever people accept innovations that their neighbors (however that is defined) have made as improvements in carrying out their daily tasks. The rate of cultural change may be so slow as to be almost imperceptible. It may speed up with population increase or decrease or with changes in the environment, including the social environment. It may go absolutely wild if novelty is valued for itself.

Cultural change can be divided into two categories: change by increment, which is relatively slow, can be called "development." It is the means by which people fine-tune their tools and meanings. The second is change by disaster, which may result from many external causes: from events in the physical environment such as earthquakes or volcanic eruptions, or from biological events like epidemics of disease (granting the cultural dimension of disease), or from social events like revolution, conquest, colonialism, or political collapse.[1] Incremental changes are usually comfortable and may even go unnoticed. Disasters, however, are never comfortable and are almost always remembered as "the day things changed."

SOME CHALLENGES

Anthropology was late in coming to the study of cultural change. It took many decades to learn that cultures were not even stable, let alone static—that those are labels that simplify description.

However in the early 1930s anthropologists, observing the impact of Western conquest on the non-Western world, found that if one aspect of a cultural tradition was disturbed, other aspects would in turn be disturbed. That observation was over-generalized into the doctrine of "cultures as wholes." A favorite image was a string of beads—if you pick up one bead, all of the other beads move. As far as I can find, everybody focused on the beads and nobody asked about the string.

About the same time, anthropologists realized that contradictions can occur within a culture if the contradictory elements do not turn up in the same context. Fundamentalist Christian faith often coexists with a belief in astrology, which is a modern manifestation of pre-Christian religious notions from classical Greece and the ancient Near East. Some people today subscribe to both belief systems, finding no difficulty in keeping them in separate compartments of their lives so that the contradictions are never relevant.

Still in the same decade—the 1930s—studies began to focus on cultural change (called *acculturation* in the United States and *culture contact* in Britain). The American Anthropological Association appointed a blue-ribbon committee to examine whether their journal, *The American Anthropologist*, should be allowed to publish articles on acculturation. Differences of opinion rang loud—was acculturation a legitimate part of anthropology or should collection of memory cultures continue to dominate it? Fortunately for themselves and the discipline, the committee decided than such studies were permissible. Their decision had little to do with any interest in how culture works—they still focused on the destruction or warping of "stable" aboriginal cultures. It was nevertheless an important step in the history of anthropology because it turned us from a focus on precontact culture to a focus on conditions actually met in the field.

After World War II and the emergence of the so-called "Third World," acculturation studies gave way to "development" studies.

The global relevance of these ideas became apparent far beyond anthropology.

Today we are again faced with redefining the task—to discover the devices by which culture grows or adapts to new situations. In the 1950s, linguistics was breaking away from its behaviorist period. The linguists' emerging questions centered around how utterances—specifically sentences—were created. Noam Chomsky asked: how could a child understand or utter sentences that had never been said before? He and his colleagues postulated an underlying scheme of grammatical rules as part of the human genetic endowment—a scheme that, within limits, can be superficially shaped into different languages. In this view, all real-world languages are manifestations of the human genetic template for "language."

Today cultural anthropologists are beginning to ask that same kind of question. Linguists were concerned with discovering how sentences were formed when people speak and how people can understand sentences never before uttered. An analogous, but more difficult, question is: how can people manipulate culture they have not been taught to deal with? How do they develop new culture?

The challenge to cultural anthropology is there to see: is there a "grammar" of culture hidden from our view as the grammar of language was hidden before Panini or before Chomsky? Are there cultural equivalents of the grammatical "parts of speech"? If so, what tasks do such "parts of culture" perform, as verbs indicate actions and nouns indicate things? How do we distinguish the quasi-grammatical structure of culture (if there is one) from its qualitative dimension?

We must learn as much as we can from linguists (or anybody else) who have been asking that kind of questions for several decades. But it is equally important to note that the linguistic models cannot be transferred wholesale to the consideration of cultural problems. Language, complex though it undoubtedly is, is simple compared to culture.

The questions for students of culture are difficult:

• Does culture-as-a-whole exist, or is the idea merely an over-simple conceit that was once useful to anthropologists? Is such an idea still useful as we examine large-scale multiethnic or multicultural societies—those that are held together by glue like money or contract law instead of by the mechanical solidarity that our ancestors (and perhaps we ourselves when young) found within small-scale unicultural groups?

• Does an idea of culture as a set of processes fit with ideas of cultures-as-wholes?

• Although the idea of "a culture" is probably here to stay, did anthropology go seriously wrong early in the twentieth century when it added the "a," as it were, and began to deal with separate cultures separately? When today's anthropologists rail against the idea of culture, do they mean "culture" generically or "a culture" specifically?

• How are cultural contradictions dealt with within cultures? By students of cultures?

• How do children (or adults, for that matter) learn their culture? Is everything they learn a part of their culture?

• What are the limits beyond which culture, or any specific cultural tradition, cannot be stretched and still be acceptable to people as self-consistent?

The challenge for today's anthropologists is to drag the sacred premises of conventional anthropology into the open and reexamine them. Of course, this is what postmodern anthropologists are doing, although some of them seem to turn their backs on old problems simply because they are old. Perhaps the wheel has to be discovered anew by each generation just to keep the wheel current. However, the older generation cannot help pointing out that what they are saying is for the most part not new, but merely stated in new terminology, using different philosophers and different metaphors. Can anybody supply a context within which older and newer ideas can be compared? There is less real progress than there seems to be.

Here I can deal with only two aspects of these oversized problems. My premise is that a theory of culture is as good as its capacity to deal with orderly growth and emendation on the one hand, and with turbulence and disaster on the other.

• Can ideas of transformation, as that term has been used in physics, linguistics, the study of myth, and the study of performance, be adapted to understanding cultural dynamics?

• Can ideas of "recontexting"—taking ideas or things out of one cultural context and inserting them into another—be used to arrive at a better understanding of "cultures-as-wholes"?

Neither of these questions here assumes an outside cultural influence. We shall deal with outside factors later in the book, in Chapter 9.

TRANSFORMATION

Transformation is a treacherous idea because it has come to mean so many different things to so many researchers with so many different concerns. Each area of research *may* make a contribution to understanding transformation in the normal day-to-day workings of a culture, but the idea as it is used in those various other disciplines does not fit cultural studies precisely. The misfit becomes apparent as we examine transformation in physics, linguistics, and mythology.

Physics. Physics is, in many ways, about the processes involved in transformation of *matter*. Some of the problems underlying thermodynamics, which is about the rules governing the transformo of heat into energy and/or energy into heat, are instructive. Adapting thermodynamic ideas to the study of culture is limited by a very simple fact: nobody has yet figured out what might be the cultural equivalent of heat or energy. The idea of heat was transformed by Galileo into the more refined and useable idea of temperature. Temperature can be more easily measured. In order to measure it, however, somebody had to invent a scale. In 1742, the Swedish astronomer Anders Celsius did just that: he took the freezing point of water and called it *zero*. He took the boiling point of water and called it *100*. He then divided the difference into a hundred segments that he called *degrees*. It was an astonishing act of creativity.

The idea of heat was (although not changed) now enlarged to include the idea of quantifiable temperature. A scale was then invented so that the heat of one substance could be compared with the heat of another. The next step demanded the idea that is now called "thermodynamic temperature," with its unit, the

Kelvin (which means temperature expressed as totally indepen-dent of any substances that exhibit the temperature)—again, a creative leap to the temperature scale on which vapor, water, and ice can all be expressed together.

My point is that the concepts of heat, temperature, thermody-namic temperature—and all the other ideas of thermodynamics—had to be created by observers on the basis of observed characteristics displayed by bodies with different characteristics of heat and energy.

Nobody has yet found the "heat" or the "energy" in cultural matters. The problem of observing cultural matters and compar-ing them meaningfully with other cultural matters is beset by far greater cultural and psychological blocks than is the observation of heat in matter.

From these examples from physics, it becomes apparent that we need quantifiable *analogues* to cultural phenomena. Some cultural matters can be statisticized (but we must always remem-ber to ask—with what significance?) and some can be expressed in a sort of algebra (which may or may not help). But the ana-logues—the concepts of "cultural temperature" to refine our perceptions of "cultural heat"—have not yet appeared. This is one of the most pressing problems for the next generation of anthropologists, and the difficulties are profound. Anthropolo-gists could, for example, model a curve for cultural change by creating variables that would make it possible to quantify tech-nological change—say by the rate of patents (which, would, of course, block out the possibility of significant comparison). Whenever they do, however, they have to be very careful that they are not snookered by the idea dimensions of culture changes, or by the important areas of the culture under study that they have omitted in order to get a measure. We might bor-row techniques and insights from other social scientists, but I believe I am right that all of them have either forgotten or defined away vast areas of culture from the measures they have created. Those excluded areas may return as monsters to plague their systems. I repeat—it won't be easy.

Linguistics. We have already noted that the word transformation, and ideas that go with it, transformed the study of language in the

1950s and 1960s. Noam Chomsky created something he called transformational grammar.[2] He first figured out the linear structure of a sentence—a sort of action chain. How does selection of one sentence element limit or direct what a speaker can select as the next elements if a sentence is to be understood? A necessary first step is to determine what Chomsky called "phrase structure rules," which are rules for generating the parts of understandable sentences. What are the ways and degrees to which the first selected elements of a sentence determine, or at least influence, selection of later elements in the same sentence?

The concept of transformational grammar can then be added: this sets forth rules for turning declarative statements into negatives, questions, passives, and the like. Transformational grammar is a set of rules in the same sense that the laws of thermodynamics are a set of rules. The former seem to me to be more complicated because linguists must work in two arenas: a system of sounds that must carry a system of meaning. The way the sound system and the meaning system fit together has, for many decades, been a challenging question. Understanding the way structural components and transformational components work together to produce both systems is equally challenging.

The concept of transformational grammar, like thermodynamics, can be mathematized—indeed, it seems to have grown out of mathematical logic, which Chomsky knew in one area—philosophy—and was able to import (this can be called recontexting) into another area—linguistics. One must first transform the ideas into elements that can be mathematized, which is itself an act of great cultural creativity.

In cultural matters, something similar (but far more complex) is happening: perceptual data, premises and values, and a tool kit all have input into an information base. That base is used for both thinking and doing. The two (thinking and doing) lead to the two aspects of culture we have discussed earlier in this book: the internal aspect, which some scholars have called mentifacts, and the external aspects of culture, which are artifacts—tools, products, ways of behaving.

Is it feasible (in analogy, or in response to some proved or some mystical association between language and culture) to postulate or look for genetic rules that underlie the organization of aspects of culture other than language? The basic questions are:

• What is the relationship between language and the rest of culture? Arguments about whether language is a part of culture or something separate (but nevertheless intimately related to culture) are no longer enough.

• Are the workings of one of the two (say, language) reflected in the workings of the other (culture)? This was the question posed by Sapir and Whorf.[3]

• Is there a grammar underlying culture in the sense that there is a grammar of sentences? Is there a genetic substate or template that provides a limitation on the way cultures change and develop?

Myth. As far as I am aware, Vladimir Propp's idea of story processes[4] was the first step toward a study of transformation in the realm of myth and story. Propp established the equivalent of Chomsky's phrase-structure rules—a trajectory that underlies one set of fairy tales. He has been roundly condemned because his trajectory applies only to the stories he considered—condemned by people who could more profitably have been looking for the trajectories of other sets of stories and trying to figure out a more general statement of the principles he discovered.

Are there rules for permuting story? What is the association between story and the rest of a human life? the rest of a culture? Do we *always* force our perceptions and our behavior into the terms of stories we already know? Is it possible to teach our students not to do it? To examine their own story anew every time they hear a story? Is it possible to make up a new story that is not a variation of some other story?

One way to learn more about how culture works is to expand our understanding of transformation.

RECONTEXTING

Recontexting may well be a form of transformation. However, it deserves separate treatment to avoid confusion with what other scholars have claimed was transformation. Recontexting, obviously, is lifting something out of one context and depositing it in another.

What, then, is a context? The dictionary says that the word *context* comes from the past participle of the Latin verb *contexere*, "to weave together," and means the interrelated circumstances in which an event occurs, or the part or passages that surround the word or topic specifically being studied. *Contextual* is an adjective meaning that the topic (noun) depends on its context. *To contextualize* is to put something into its appropriate context.

The first feature of recontexting is that a piece of culture—an idea or a concept or a tool—can be learned in one context and then applied in quite another. Such an operation is the essence of one sort of creativity. The operation is also significant in creating a "whole" culture in which one part is intimately related to other parts.

An immense amount of cultural growth and innovation is carried out in the form of recontexting as meanings are transferred from one range within a particular cultural tradition to another within the same cultural tradition. Indeed, putting ideas from one context into another, then organizing and working through and explaining what changes they work in the new context, may be one of the major forms of creativity. Recontexting either uses or creates bridges from one zone of a culture to another. It makes the various zones of a culture consonant with one another. In short, it is one mechanism for creating "the whole."

In its new context, however, the old idea may be wholly innovative. The newly recontexted element is almost surely not a total or complete duplication of the original—only parts of it will be relevant in the new context. It may not even be accurate from the standpoint of the original context. The new context almost always demands reconsideration of old meanings. (The new meanings may then feed back into the original context, making changes there.)

I first realized the importance of recontexting when, in 1950, I watched Tiv consciously seek in the nonjural reaches of their own culture for guiding principles to be used in their traditional moots as well as in the courts that had been introduced in Nigeria by the British colonial administration.[5] It became evident that the Tiv were creating law by taking some of their customs out of one context and then reformulating them as a guide for management of conflict in a foreign system—the courts that had been established according to the practices of the British colonial overlords.

Law can occasionally be original; it may sometimes even be used as a vehicle for innovation. But if the law is out of phase with the rest of the culture, it is likely either to be ignored or to become tyrannical. The processes of creative lawmaking are the processes of refining ideas within a jural context that are consonant with other versions of those ideas originally developed in other dimensions of the same culture. Developed political systems have a set of specialized institutions (legislatures) that are charged with creating the reformulations, and another set of institutions concerned with managing their application (courts).

Many ideas or artifacts thus have two or more contexts within a culture, and a few may dominate almost all its contexts.[6] Such ideas are likely to have somewhat different meanings and very different uses in each context. Law and religion, for example, must both be concerned with most of the other realms of both social and intellectual life. The two are closely consonant with one another in spite of the fact that the courts and the legislature may be in conflict with one another, and either or both may be in conflict with organized religious bodies. Both law and religion thus add new dimensions and new metaphors, as well as new conflicts, to their common themes.

It soon became evident that the recontexting process, having been found active in the law, was to be found rampant in almost all reaches of every culture. Recontexting is one of the major processes by which culture grows and is kept consistent. Its simplicity is astonishing.

In searching to solve problems in Context 2, people take leads from other dimensions of their culture (Context 1). An idea from Context 1 is recognized as cogent to the new situation; it is purposely put into a situation in which it can be further redefined and enlarged. It can then be restated in a new context. In this process, the ideas cross a sort of threshold into a creative area that can be compared to the threshold state of the rites-of-passage trajectory. In this creative area, they are adjusted and reinterpreted before they are fed back into the problem context (see Figure 6–1).

Recontexting thus means that an idea taken from one part or context of a culture is specifically edited, then applied in a different context within the same culture. Good serviceable myth, for

FIGURE 6–1

A Simplified General Model of Recontexting

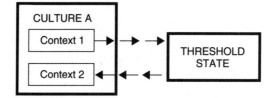

example, has an important place in ritual, but the ideas that underlie the myth are also recontexted into politics and economics; they may even go into the theater so that the audience can understand them in story form and bring them up to date.

To sum up, comparatively little law arises in a purely legal context. The sources of law are to be found in the customs within other institutions of society and in the ideas and values that underlie those institutions. The commercial code of our own law, for example, is a restatement of part of what our people generally agree is moral business practice. Some parts—probably a small part—of that practice are edited and recontexted into the statutes. The new context is the specialized institution (courts) by which people can see to it that others carry out their businesses according to the statutes, which means according to acceptable practice. The same ideas have one context in the institutions of business and, somewhat edited, another in context of the courts. The binding agent of "cultures-as-wholes" turns out to be the recontexting process.

Play. The second feature of recontexting is that either it resembles play or it is play. Play is hard to define because there are no more fundamental qualities to which it can be reduced. The *World Book Dictionary* gives seventeen basic meanings of *play*, only one of them obsolete. The third edition of the *American Heritage Dictionary* gives thirteen meanings of *play* as an intransitive verb; fourteen more as a transitive verb, and ten as a noun—before it ventures into a large number of idioms. The *Oxford English Dictionary* fills eighteen finely packed columns on the topic.

Play is (whatever else it is) one way of recontexting ideas from their original context into a new context. Consider the rules within the play context that differ from the rules of the original, non-play context. In play, unlike real life, the rules *must* be accepted and carefully followed. A game like baseball has very specific rules that define the game *as a game*, smaller in scope than real life. Within the context established by those rules, only the game matters; the rest of life is shut out. It is a finable offense to allow rage from real life to overflow into the game—as a player, you can't shout profanities at the umpire and get away with it. Yet the game reflects some of our most valued ideas about what real life is about. Within the game, the goals are reduced to the achievable—if you are skillful enough, have good enough teammates, and follow the rules, you can win.

This recontexting quality of play—taking a small slice of life and reestablishing it in a special situation—is the essence of creativity. Play is a way to lift ideas out of their original context so that they can be developed in a new way in a new context, free of the burdens and limitations imposed by the context from which they stemmed. We not only play games; both babies and adults play with words. Children play house. From time to time in our lives, we play at love or at work.

The scientific investigation of play began in the last part of the nineteenth century and was brought neatly to summary in a serious and boring book by Groos in 1898.[7] That book said firmly that play is a make-believe area (that is, a restricted context) in which the young can safely practice the skills that they will need in order to survive as adults in the real world. Recent studies of play among nonhuman primates have underscored Groos's insights. Among rhesus monkeys, most of the play among juveniles consists of play-chases and play-fights. In this play, the young monkeys learn how to bite without being bitten, and how to evade pursuers. Ultimately they will need these skills to see them through fights for social rank and position and also to escape danger from predators.[8]

This does not mean that every aspect of an animal's adult behavior is first practiced as play. Nor does it mean that play is limited to skills to be used in adult behavior. Lions, for example, have a reputation of being playful animals; they use any of several signs to tell one another that their acts are to be taken as play. One lion may approach another with exaggerated bounds; like some other animals, notably dogs, they indicate readiness to play by lowering the front part of the body; they may roll on their backs; or they may nip at or push another lion. Like monkeys, lions have a facial expression, which ethologists call a "play face," that indicates the special context of play. Lion play, like monkey play, sometimes gets rough.[9]

Gregory Bateson went to the zoo in search of animal behavior that would indicate that an animal understood certain acts as a sign that its behavior was to be understood differently in the present context than in other contexts. He found his answer in a gesture that many animals use that means "What I am about to do, I do in play." That gesture is a sign understood by other animals of the same species. The signal means, "These actions in which we now engage do not denote what those actions *for which they stand* would denote in other contexts." The playful nip denotes the bite, "but it does not denote what would be denoted by the bite."[10] In other words, the meaning of acts is different in a play context from what it would be in other contexts.

If the play is aggressive, what is the boundary between serious aggression and play-fighting? How are the two contexts bound together by a recontexted idea or action, at the same time that the recontexted idea has limitations put on it in each of its new contexts?

Human beings play not only for the sake of learning techniques for survival, although they probably do that. Perhaps more important, they play for the sake of cultural survival and enrichment—they play at being cultured. You can play house, play store, play king, play priest. You can even play God.

Any part of a culture can be taken from its original sphere into a sphere that resembles play. The sphere of play is always marked by a condensed set of rules. Play shares with art the importance of rules within which it must occur.

One reason television is such a powerful tool for education is that it changes the context: it takes some culture out of the "real" world and puts it in a box. Looking at television, you can stand aside from life and watch it. The basic problem that television has introduced is to make us aware that much of real life is boring and without story. Television has to exaggerate movement and constantly rev up the viewers' emotions in order to retain its audience. When the viewers reflect the revved-up versions back into their so-called real-world context, the culture in that real world seems to them bland and namby-pamby—and so the temptation to rev "reality" up may become overwhelming.

The third statement we can make is that art, writing, education, simulation—even planning—are all modes of recontexting. Writing takes meaning out of its aural context and turns it into equivalent phenomena in the visual context. Some people have trouble learning to make this contextual shift—so-called dyslexia. Certainly many people consider information from the two sources to be somewhat different in kind. Being literate changes the way we look at everything around us.

Art. Art too is a process of recontexting. Using a combination of three elements—play, symbols, and explanation—a painter or playwright can release ideas from his or her unconscious to use for creative purposes. To do that, he or she needs a safe place in which to play—a kind of threshold state—to allow the vision to emerge so that it can be put into its new context without fear. This kind of creativity not only resembles play—it *is* a kind of play. But it is also a way of recontexting—daring to put an idea into a new context, to see it in a new way, and perhaps to change everything in the process. If the limin of this play-like context is not there, creativity stays under wraps.

Thus play, or something like it, is an essential part of all art—indeed, of much learning. The artist must either have or must dare to create a safe place to think "unthinkable" thoughts, and to express them in a way that allows people back in real life to expand their appreciation of the human condition. Artists are sometimes considered dangerous—they dare to question received ways, and they dare to play with the most serious subjects. They dare to recontext our ordinary ideas into totally extraordinary ideas.

Art also finds a way to create an explanatory context by allowing us to think and feel several things at once. In that way, we can see, sometimes in one illuminating moment, how everything fits together. The recontexting of art turns cultures into wholes.

Education. Education, if it is done right, is itself a realm that allows us to do our recontexting—a safe limin within which to learn about our cultural ideas and their history, and in which we can dare to question them. Education is quite different from indoctrination. Schools or their equivalent do indeed have to indoctrinate us with the ideas of our forebears and our contemporaries. But good schools also teach us to recontext the ideas with which we are indoctrinated, and they offer us the threshold state where it is safe to recontext those ideas. The task of students is to recontext some of what they learn in school into the real world. In the process, we learn recontexting—and in *that* process we learn to question our premises about the nature of ourselves and our neighbors and our communities, including the global society. Schools that supply only answers turn out crippled human beings.

Simulation. Simulation is a form of recontexting for tactical purposes. Tabletop war games and computer modeling allow us to recontext many elements so that we don't have to live through something in order to know a little bit about how it will come out. Then we don't have to experience something before we can do it—we can do it right the first time.

Planning. Planning, which is a special form of simulation, means figuring things out in a hypothetical context so that the "real-life" context will not be affected unless, as a matter of policy, you want specifically to introduce the lessons from the smaller, safer context into the larger context.

Recontexting cultural information is creative—and it is one way that cultures as wholes are formed and maintained. It is also a technique that should (but too often fails to) enrich the analyses of anthropologists. Without successful recontexting, cultural traditions can wind their way to insurmountable cultural traps.

Chapter 7

Pattern and Turbulence

People perceive cultural dynamics primarily in the form of stories. The art of the historian is the art of turning recorded past events into stories. Religion is often, and most convincingly, wrapped in stories. Every person's life can be told as a story—indeed, several stories. Epics, biographies, histories, or jokes all amuse and instruct us. An important component of the art of science writing is turning mathematics into stories. The most gripping stories are those that first threaten the underlying pattern, then relieve tension and console us by confirming that pattern. Stories will be examined in Chapter 12, in a discussion of how we work with culture. But here, the important point is the patterns that lie behind the stories.

Stories—and histories—do not repeat themselves; each one is different. But the patterns that undergird stories turn up again and again.[1]

The art of the ethnographer is to learn, then to translate, a foreign people's stories without inserting his or her own pattern. To do that you have to make the pattern underlying your own story overt so that the pattern underlying the foreign story can be grasped. Today's ethnographers sometimes report both patterns at once; it is called the reflexive mode of reporting ethnography, and when it works it is most instructive. But it may not work if the ethnographer gets lost in his or her autobiographical adventures and loses sight of both patterns.

The art of the cultural anthropologist—the next step after the ethnographic facts are gathered—involves sternly resisting the temptation to succumb to *any* specific pattern, including his or her own. Doing that allows us to recognize that the stories of our own culture are just stories like those of any other culture. The discipline comes in being sure that the pattern underlying our own stories—or our own theories—does not sneak in through the back door. One of the major flaws in social science occurs when a scientist allows a culture-bound story—or, more often, a theory developed in his own society or his own discipline—to become the basis for comparison. The Napoleonic code or Roman law or the common law cannot provide the theoretical basis for comparative law. Rather, they are important *examples*, but the patterns within them are very likely not to fit the ethnographic facts gathered in other places or at other times. It is unwise to shove parakeets into pigeonholes.

Once that realization is achieved, and only then (it is difficult and has to be achieved over and over again, every time your work with new material), the anthropologist can proceed to the pattern behind the patterns—that is, he can compare the patterns that underlie both stories and theories from many different peoples.

STORY AND THEORY

Scientists are moved and limited by the stories of their own cultures—but also by the theories of their disciplines. Those theories behave much like stories. Theories, however, differ from other stories in that they are undergirded by some method like mathematics or step-by-step computer programming so that strict canons of proof can be applied. The characters in theoretical stories are neurons and electrons, or genes and chromosomes and gametes. The characters in the stories of theory in social science are human acts and ideas and the patterns they form. A cultural theory tells the story of the regularities of events or behavior under given conditions, and how events or behavior change with altered conditions.

Theories are thus descriptions of patterns, sometimes highly mathematized. Models and simulations also, of course, follow patterns. The models presented in this study are all, in fact, patterns. Such patterns are not "mere stories" (perhaps no story should be described as "mere"), yet they work like stories in that they provide overt matrices into which specific incidents can be arranged in a familiar way—first threatening the pattern but ultimately strengthening it.

Scientists are trained to give up theories if they do not accommodate all the observed action. Giving up a theory may be an act of heroism—one's life has been invested in it. In fact, giving up any pattern may be an act of heroism.

PATTERN

The word *pattern* has an honorable, if shaky, history in early anthropology. It means an arrangement of parts or elements, with emphasis on "arrangement." In my search for the origins of the idea of pattern in anthropology, I first went to Ruth Benedict's *Patterns of Culture*.[2] She does not discuss pattern at all and certainly does not define it. The same is true for several other authors with whom I associated the word. I did not search exhaustively, but I could not find a discussion of pattern in the early literature of anthropology.

I did learn, however, that the word *pattern* ultimately goes back to the Latin word for *father*, and that a pattern is an archetype—a consistent, characteristic form—that is worthy of being followed. All sorts of activities may conform to a pattern—making a dress or a suit, or landing an airplane, or analyzing the degree of expertise with which an individual marksman hits a target. A pattern may be an arrangement of forms or components, but it is the *arrangement* rather than the specific components that creates the pattern.

A pattern is a guide or prototype—it not only underlies story (a way of structuring overt events) but can also be an arrangement of emotions or social processes that allows us to understand them better by putting them into a more generalized context.

If a pattern persists, we are gratified, both emotionally and intellectually. It has been postulated that when our senses perceive the fit of perception with pattern, our brains get a little shot of endorphin. Yet almost surely the patterns themselves are not a genetic part of the human being.

Every culture is encapsulated in its patterns—and in its stories. Benedict's achievement in *Patterns of Culture* was not actually to point out the *idea* of pattern, but rather to develop and illuminate the idea that there are *Leitmotiven* in some cultures, and that the *Leitmotiv*, once discerned, allows the anthropologist to discover the pattern in the factual material about that culture and to describe it in the most elegant form.

Some stories can release the mind from some of the strictures that other patterns have fastened on it. You can think many thoughts in the play-like form of stories that you dare not think in real life. Moreover, stories, perhaps more effectively than any other mode, allow people to examine and question the basic premises of their culture. We can take ideas from almost anywhere and cast them as versions of a story, either to underscore traditional values or to question those values with bold new propositions.

Because of their reassuringly familiar patterns, stories are devices not only for organizing but also for transforming and recontexting many of the familiar events of living. When we tell stories (or create dynamic models), we set events into a realm that resembles play. There we can draw tight boundaries around them. Everything not in the story becomes momentarily irrelevant. Everything not in the pattern can (for the moment, at least) be safely ignored. In the acts of transforming experience or data into story, we have established a way to comment on the reality that has been excluded from the pattern of the story.

Thus, successful storytellers arrange the events of a story in a recognized pattern, even if that pattern has never been made overt; the analogy to grammar is tempting but almost surely oversimplifies the process. Storytellers do not stop to explain themselves. Explanations (including everything that happened before the story begins, called *back-story*) have no place in most stories— they stop the forward drive and, paradoxically, obscure the pattern precisely by dwelling on it. A good storyteller just lets the pattern unfold. That means letting the *story* unfold the very while that original or recontexted ideas enrich its pattern. The more elements of a culture can be included in the story, the more interesting the story—and the more powerful the pattern.

TURBULENCE

The power of a pattern is perceived in the discomfort or worse that erupts when it is disturbed. The expected flow of events, or of the story, either peters out or is suddenly shattered by something that has no place in the pattern. Only with the failure of a pattern can one fully realize the power of that pattern.

Equilibrium. No discussion of pattern can overlook the tricky idea of equilibrium. The regular flow of a cultural pattern has sometimes been called *equilibrium* by analogy to the use of that word in physical sciences and electric engineering. But *equilibrium* is a deceptive word: in physics it means a system in which all the vectors equalize one another in such a way that there is no torque in any axis. In chemistry, it means that forward and reverse reactions occur at equal rates, thereby giving the impression that nothing is happening. In social science it has too often been confused with a "normal" state—even a static state. But processes are at work to maintain any equilibrium. Discovering the processes is the goal of every science.

Cultural equilibrium would thus seem to be a state in which all the ongoing cultural processes are counteracted by other ongoing processes. That does not necessarily mean that no change is occurring, but only that a change is counteracted by another change so that there is no immediate evidence of change. The idea of cultural equilibrium was, it seems to me, a bridge across which anthropologists could get from their old view of the rigidity of custom to the newer view that not all processes are immediately evident. The idea may well be an illusion created by too literal analogies to physics and engineering. It is difficult to study equilibrium—primarily because systems show up to fieldworkers not so much when they are working well as when they are disturbed, whereupon everybody becomes aware of how they *should* be working. The link between "equilibrium" and "should be so" turns out to be treacherous indeed.

———————————

Cultural turbulence. When a disturbance of pattern erupts, people are left casting about, not knowing what may happen next or what to do next. Cultural turbulence feels like violent agitation or disturbance; chaos or restlessness; unrest. Durkheim and his colleagues called it *anomie.*[3] People almost surely first struggle to reestablish the old pattern. However, that very attempt creates an awareness of the old pattern—it brings it, so to speak, out of the preconscious and into the conscious. With this new realization of the pattern, people are able to examine and evaluate it. They may well, given the new context and the new awareness, consciously decide that there are better ways to overcome or override the disorientation of the disturbed pattern than by trying to reinforce it.

Turbulence thus means the interruption of the flow of the pattern. It may imply violent agitation from a lack of perceived pattern, or it may imply simple unrest and unruliness. In physics the term has the special meaning of *turbulent flow*, which describes a situation in which local velocities and pressures within a total flow oscillate randomly. From an anthropological stance, it implies a feeling of being lost—not knowing what to do when the culture fails.

Turbulence and cultural change are not the same thing, for all that cultural change may engender turbulence. Cultural change is more complex—it involves alteration either of the meanings in peoples' heads or of the artifacts they use and the behavior they perform and expect. But some cultural traditions, at some stages, exhibit ongoing, repetitive turbulence as part of their patterns. Turbulence can even be a part of equilibrium—in which case, it is probably not perceived as turbulence. Thus, turbulence *per se* does not necessarily involve the kind of alteration that is implicit in situations of culture change. Turbulence can be domesticated—introduced into a culture pattern as a permanent and repetitive part of it. It may not be comfortable, but nevertheless it is expected, and because it is part of the pattern people know what to do with it.

The distinctions that have been drawn here are summarized in Figure 7–1.

FIGURE 7–1

Some Useful Distinctions for Examining Culture at Work

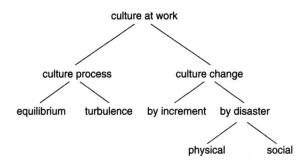

Having seen how action chains form and how they change, and having examined the nature of turbulence, our next steps are to discover the processes by which simultaneously ongoing action chains interlink over time, to ask how feedback affects the inter-linkages, and to further explore the idea of turbulence.

My analyses here are again built on insights derived from Michael Thompson.[4] He overlapped his event chain about rubbish and durable goods (Figure 7–2a) with Marx's views (turned into an event chain) about the production and consumption cycle (Figure 7–2b). The process that returns some material from consumption to production is at least as complex as the process that

FIGURE 7–2a

The Rubbish Cycle

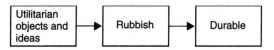

FIGURE 7–2b

Marx's Production and Consumption Cycle

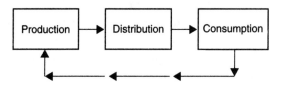

FIGURE 7–3

Production, Distribution, and Rubbish

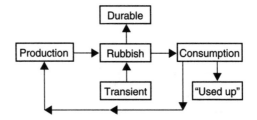

rescues some items from the rubbish heap and endows them with durable value. Much of the material may "get lost" in this process, but some is actually returned so that the whole makes a cycle.

Thompson then superimposed the two models. The result is shown in Figure 7–3.

The cell in the middle, which would be "rubbish" in one chain and "distribution" in the other, has been left blank. It is the threshold space (*la marge*, in van Gennep's expressive original term) where the two processes meet—the site of whatever adjustments are required.

To explain what happens when several processes are going on at the same time—and thus to begin the illumination of some complex cyclical social processes—Thompson used both Waddington's topographic concepts[5] and René Thom's topological geometry.[6] Although the examples that follow build on Thompson's ideas (and, less directly, on Waddington and Thom), the models in the rest of this chapter are based on my fieldwork among the Tiv of north-central Nigeria in 1949–1953.

Tiv, during the early years of the twentieth century, experienced a series of antiwitchcraft movements that the British colonial administration tried desperately to control, never realizing that they were themselves a major part of the problem instead of the solution. To analyze a situation, one must unpack the native perceptions by seeing them as several processes that have been congregated into a single set of activities. That is how Tiv went about changing leaders in the early part of this century. The dynamics of the Tiv political system provide an illuminating example of the way complex ideas[7] can relate several action chains into a single set of cycles.

Tiv did not indigenously recognize political offices as such, but rather ran their polity by a delicate balance of lineages at several levels of size and complexity.[8] They did use some honorific titles, especially in the Eastern part of Tivland. Those titles had been borrowed from the neighboring Jukun, and were surrounded with some pomp, but among Tiv no actual authority ever inhered in them. The British colonial administration, however, could not begin to imagine ruling without a hierarchy of officials, with themselves at the top. They also assumed that what they knew about the Jukun applied, unchanged, to Tiv. They therefore appointed officials—chiefs, policemen, messengers, court officials—who could apply sanctions. Under the guidance of a policy called "indirect rule," they did it on what they mistakenly understood to be the principles of Tiv society. Their policy, however, gave new substance to those Jukun-derived titles.

Tiv had to adjust to the fact that the colonial administration not only required "responsible"[9] native officials but also insisted to itself that these officials derived from indigenous patterns, which they did not. The officials whom the administration described by Tiv (or Jukun) words were sometimes associated with lineage groups that *were* indeed recognized by Tiv. However, any association of authority and of tasks associated with those titles was fabricated (unwittingly) by the colonial officials.

Tiv nurture a deep suspicion of powerful people. Their indigenous political system recognized no status whatever in which power or authority inhered by right. However, a community of a million people[10] cannot be held together and made to work without a power structure. That power structure has to be maintained; positions within it have to be filled and refilled. Succession has to occur.

Western democratic systems have built mechanisms such as elections (held either on a calendar basis or when the party in power loses its majority) into their overt political processes in order to achieve it. Periodic replacement occurs in overt, prescribed action chains. But when, as among the Tiv, succession is *not* explicit, and the mechanism is *not* socially agreed upon, succession may take place by the recurrent reappearance of an excluded monster—that is, something denied or thrust out of awareness which nevertheless figures in determining the action chains. The Tiv device for changing the personnel while maintaining the system is such an excluded monster.

During the period of colonial government (and something similar seems to have happened earlier), witchcraft charges were commonly made as a means of changing the political slate. That is, the current leaders would be charged with witchcraft. This meant not only that Tiv turned on them but also that they could no longer perform the tasks that the so-called Native Administration thought were their "responsibility." They were therefore replaced.

That is, government-backed actions by persons chosen by the Native Administration were often resented by many Tiv who were not officeholders. Charges of what Westerners might call tyranny would spring up—but Tiv used the idiom of witchcraft to describe such tyranny. The people would demand that the witches be stopped—which was their idiom for demanding a change (process X-Y-Z in Figure 7–4).

The excluded monster was an expression, in witchcraft terms, of what we might call a mystical or imaginary action chain. That is, Tiv expressed their sense of injustice and their fear of tyranny in an idiom of witchcraft and cannibalism. The hidden premise is that nobody can become truly outstanding or more successful than his or her neighbors without witchcraft. Whenever powerful people began to throw their weight around, Tiv said they were using witchcraft to accomplish private ends.

Tiv perceived the situation this way: in a well-run society, they stated, the land must be repaired by day and also by night. In their idiom, repairing the land by day meant calling together the elders of the community in moots; the deliberations of those elders would maintain peace and prosperity. Repairing the land at night, on the other hand, kept society in line with the universe;

FIGURE 7–4

Action Chain for Replacing Leaders Among Tiv

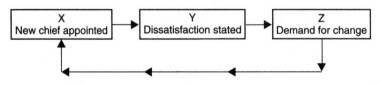

it demanded secret ritual, and was said to involve removing bodies from graves, restoring them to demi-life, then using them as "sacrifices" in those secret rituals. By day, the powerful men who ran the moots and maintained the peace were called *mbavesen*, or elders. By night, the same men were called the *mbatsav*, those with the mystical substance *tsav* on their hearts.[11] The people involved were actually the same individuals.

This secret society of "witches" (*mbatsav*) was said to meet "at night" to perform secret ceremonies for "repairing the land." Their secret ceremonies were deemed just as important as moots and other ways of taking community decisions if the land was to be kept repaired. Tiv accounted for some natural deaths by saying that the deceased was killed by the *mbatsav* so they could revive the corpse to sacrifice in their rituals. They admitted that the *mbatsav* had a right to the necessary human sacrifices to carry out the ritual correctly, and that the persons sacrificed had to be agnatic (paternal-line) members of the lineage affected.

Every accident or illness that led to a death was interpreted as resulting from the action of the *mbatsav* at night (process A-B-C in Figure 7–5). The legitimacy of every individual death was challenged. Had the *mbatsav* actually taken *this* particular life for sacrifice? If not, why had those *mbatsav* allowed the death to occur? If so, had they picked the right person to sacrifice? Wasn't it the turn of some other group within the overall lineage? If "too many" deaths occurred, it was "obvious" (that is, it followed Tiv premises) that the *mbatsav* had exceeded their rightful duties, had developed a taste for human flesh (a metaphor meaning that they were seeking power at the expense of others), and so were killing people indiscriminately.

At this stage, the mystical action chain was added to the political chain. "Obviously," the members of the *mbatsav* had exceeded

FIGURE 7–5

The Mystical Chain of the Mbatsav

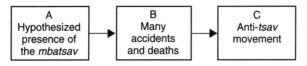

A Hypothesized presence of the *mbatsav*	B Many accidents and deaths	C Anti-*tsav* movement

their ritual requirements. Their greed had to be stopped. Thereupon a social movement would arise to root out and destroy the *mbatsav*.

Whenever any powerful people were accused of excess in any sense, then, they were called witches (*mbatsav*). As the political dissatisfaction mounted, the charges of witchcraft got louder. Countermovements arose. Revolts took the form of antiwitchcraft cults (at least so they were described by the authors of the literature and by the British administration, who were more or less the same people at that time).[12] As the cult movements were successful and spent themselves—that is, as leaders were dislodged—new elders began to consolidate their power positions. A few years later they too would be brought down—indeed, they might even be replaced by some members of the original group that the present "witches" had succeeded. Like our elections, this was a repetitive cycle that allowed for changes of officeholders. They were not recognized as such by Tiv—but they happened that way time

FIGURE 7–6

Two Interlinking Action Chains (X) and (Y) Among the Tiv

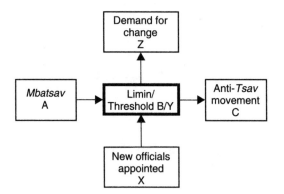

Process ABC (the moral order/chaos process): A = the *mbatsav* meet at night to perform secret ceremonies that will "make the land prosper." Their rituals to do so are said to involve a human sacrifice. B = an accident or illness that causes a death in the community (or some other anti-social event occurs); it has disappeared into limin. C = an anti-*mbatsav* movement erupts because the *mbatsav* has gone too far and endangered the community instead of repairing it.

Process XYZ (the political process) X = colonial government appoints a chief. Y = there is dissatisfaction with the actions of the chief (also disappeared into limin). Z = a demand is made for change of leadership.

after time. The specific cultural content of each cult varied, but the pattern—the action chains—remained constant.

Quite obviously, the two action chains overlap at B and Y. It can now be quite readily seen that the two trajectories have compressed themselves into a single set of events, as indicated in Figure 7–6. But, as can be seen in Figure 7–7, the two have also created a chicken-and-egg cycle of the sort that will be examined in Chapter 9.

THE CUSP

Another variable is added with another, third dimension. Figure 7–7 lies in two dimensions. In the next step of the analysis, those two dimensions are to be seen as the environment within which all the action occurs. This two-dimensional model can, in short, be considered to be a "control space"—that is, the space within which events happen. We can now add a third dimension—and, of course, we now have a three-dimensional model. The control space, however, is *not* static. Successive attempts to keep the cycle repeating precisely within that control space may well create an impact on the space itself. Because the control space is the environment of the cycling-event chain, the flat control space has to be distorted—crumpled—in order for the processes to continue

FIGURE 7–7

Process Arising from the Overlapping of the Two Trajectories of Figure 7–6

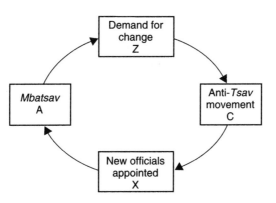

seemingly without change. The relationship of the original trajectories of Figure 7–6—ABC and XYZ—continues on a flat surface. However, if that surface is made to stand for the changing environment, the control space may not continue to be flat. As the cycle is repeated, the no-longer-flat surface of the control space may develop a steep ridge, or cusp.

If a cusp emerges on the surface of the control space, a dramatic situation is set up: two different points of view concerning the same process can now be held—one of which assumes the flat surface (what is "supposed" to happen) and the other, affected by the environment in the control space, is now crumpled and cusped, accepts the reality of what actually happens. Every fieldworker knows that when he or she asks questions, he or she is likely to get the "supposed-to" answer. Only through close and perhaps long-term observation can you actually come to understand what does in fact happen, and why it is nevertheless so important to maintain the idea of the "supposed-to."

Usually a cusp-defining event occurs when the line tracing the cycle between the supposed-to and the reality points of view reaches the cusp. However, that sudden event is *not* the destruction of the system (which it would be if only two dimensions were considered). Rather, it is a catastrophe that represents a change of dominant views: you shift from the flat-cycle control-space view to the crumpled control-space view. And now, when the cycle repeats yet again, the cusp can become an integral part of the working of the system. Many systems, it appears, have such built-in catastrophes. Catastrophes are particularly likely in the face of ambiguous meanings (like the Tiv statements about *tsav*) or of two opposed points of view (those of the Tiv and the Nature Administration).

To continue with the Tiv example: as time proceeds, the changing of the political guard takes on an appearance of catastrophe (Figure 7–8). As the cycle encounters the precipice, the tyrannous leadership is ousted by the anti-*tsav* movement. The idiom of the new cult movement that follows a few years later is not recognized by the people as a repetition of the same old cycle. They simply deplore the fact that the witches have returned and are trying to kill them again. Although the pattern is consistent, each cult is culturally perceived as different from every other cult, and none is in the idiom of politics; rather, they all involve witchcraft and healing. This means that the excluded monster of political tyranny can be kept hidden—but it reasserts itself, disguised as new witchcraft, every time the cusp is reached. Change can be built in either consciously, as with American periodic elections, or unconsciously, as with the Tiv anti-*tsav* cults.

To repeat, every time the line representing the various events in the cycling process bumps over the cusp, there is an event akin to a Thomian catastrophe—an anti-*tsav* movement. Such a catastrophe creates a sudden alteration of the appearance of the situation. Or, perhaps better put, a "new" view "wins out" over an "old" view as the process topples over the edge of the cusp. Change is now built into the process—by means of the cusp. The pattern remains unscathed.

Although it is obvious to the outside analyst that the catastrophe is a control device that keeps Tiv social structure in balance, it is not obvious to the people who live in the system, and it was certainly not obvious to the colonial administration.

As we have seen, elections are one social device for building in

FIGURE 7–8

A Cusp as Part of a Process

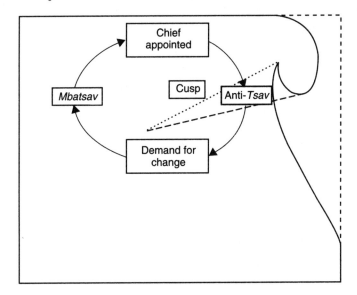

turbulence—something akin to such catastrophe—in order to control the processes purposefully. Elections provide a recurrent cusp—they bring the cusp into the open, domesticate it, and make it an overt part of the system. They are the dither mechanism—the controlled turbulence that physicists and early feedback theorists found to be required to reright the system.

By defining the cusp as the place of greatest possible variation on the cusped plane, it is possible to make some predictions about what may happen to the system when such-and-such alterations occur in the two original processes ABC and XYZ of Figure 7–6. We are not limited to what has in fact happened; the goal is to foresee all the possibilities and the effect they would have on the status quo. "Description no longer has to wait on empirical evidence: theory need no longer be constructed only in hindsight."[13] We learned enough in this way to walk on the moon the first time we tried, without having to learn by experience. Socially and culturally, we are learning to go from the level of phenomena to the level of possibility of phenomena.

Chapter 8

What Cultural Change Involves

J ust as every psychological theory demands a theory of learning, so every cultural theory demands a theory of change—development, growth, readjustment to environmental changes, and catastrophes. How is something added to the cultural tradition? How do traits get transformed? How do emphases get shifted? How does culture evolve? When it is possible to return to some *status quo ante* and when is it not possible? How do people feel about the changing culture? Under what conditions do they become disoriented by change?

All culture is changing all the time. Because no culture is ever static, any description of a culture as if it were static is misleading, because such a description ignores cultural processes and hence makes it impossible to assign cause and effect within the processes. No natural beginning point or end point of cultural change is meaningful except in the light of a specific problem. Any observer who creates a baseline either does it for a specific purpose, which should be explicitly stated, or else fails to grasp the importance of cultural process.

THE ILLUSION OF THE BASELINE

For many decades, anthropologists studying cultural change assumed they *could* discover a baseline of what a culture was like before Western contact frequently coupled with an assumption that that baseline situation was "naturally" coherent, balanced, and good. Data about these "memory cultures" were garnered by questioning old people who claimed to remember what things were like before the impact, or whose parents had told them what things were like in those days. There was, to overgeneralize, no attention paid to the biases that were systematically introduced by errors of memory or by substituting ideal for real behavior. For many of those decades, anthropologists paid no attention whatever to the situation in which their informants found themselves at the time of the interviews—that is, whether the personal or political agendas of their informants might color the views that they were ascribing to the "aboriginal" culture.

It was well known, for example, that the horse, which Plains Indian societies got by trade some time before any direct contact between them and the people who were to be their Western conquerors, totally altered the nature of Plains culture. But the fact was well known because the horse was involved in much of the warfare between the Plains peoples, and hence was of special interest to anthropologists as well as to historians. Other changes that occurred at that early time were not considered. In spite of the fact that information about some of those changes was known, little attention was paid to it because the focus was so doggedly on the changes created by European impact, and because there was a hidden premise that the culture before that impact was more or less pristine and more or less static.

This is an example of a more general problem which arises from intricacies in how anthropology works. Anthropological culture necessarily focuses on certain problems that have achieved general theoretical recognition within the discipline. It is also shaped by the context (that is, the values and concerns) of the larger world in which anthropological endeavor occurs. Contributions to the study of warfare in anthropology, for example, reflect the concern with warfare in the general Western populace.

Theoretical focus or public concern can neatly camouflage patterns or seriously limit inquiry. What Edgerton[1] calls "the myth of primitive harmony" is a fine example. As anthropologists came to understand other cultures from the standpoint of their participants, and because those other cultures survived, and because the idea of culture-as-a-whole was in the air, and because it became what we would today call "politically incorrect" to bad-mouth other groups—for all these and probably other reasons, the overgeneralization emerged not only that all cultures must be understood from the standpoint of their own premises, but also that all cultures were equally "good." It was often said that one culture was as good as another. The presence of cultural traps (not to mention the ethnocentric use of the word "harmony") was effectively hidden.

Today the idea of the baseline has reemerged in a new context: it is one of the foundations of social-impact reports. That is to say, the creator of the social-impact report purports to discover what things were like *before* some specific event, on the simplistic assumption that he or she can thereupon place the "blame" for any changes that have occurred since the time of the baseline on that specific event. It falsifies such reports in exactly the same way that the idea of a baseline turned decades of anthropological writings into inaccurate, static accounts.

REACTIONS TO CULTURAL CHANGE

Cultural change may be welcomed. For example, computers have led to vast cultural change throughout the modern world and have altered the way the world is run. Changes in the shape and size of organizations have followed. Changes in leadership patterns and in division of labor have had vast effects on traditional jobs, particularly industrial jobs, and hence on the style in which workers can live. But because computers provide new efficiencies and new careers, and because few people have experienced direct harm from them, those changes have gone largely unnoted. When the results of the way we do things with computers turn up in some distant field—employment statistics, perhaps—the relationship of cause and effect may not be immediately evident.

On the other hand, some cultural changes are painful, especially if people think their lives will be poorer or more difficult or more dangerous.

Cultural change can be divided into two sorts: change by increment, as we saw in Chapter 6, is relatively slow and long-term as people fine-tune their tools and meanings. This kind of change will be discussed in this chapter. The second is change by disaster, which is taken up in Chapters 9 and 10.

To make sense of cultural change, one must examine two factors. First, what changed on the surface? What artifacts and ideas actually changed or were replaced? Second, what sort of changes were worked in the premises, usually unconscious, that underlie people's deeds and explanations?

The vital dimension of time must also be considered in looking at both questions. How long does it take for a cultural innovation to take hold? What historical processes are involved? How long do the results of any situations created by disasters last? Do disasters permanently alter the situation or do they merely lead to suffering or inconvenience?

There are also profound considerations about whose viewpoint is taken when change is examined. The people undergoing the changes have one view—the folk-system view for which anthropologists have coined the ugly word *emic*. Because it is always at the level of experience that culture change is judged by the people undergoing it, the emotions of temporary discombobulation and permanent cultural change may seem to be the same: fear, uncertainty, anger, greed.

Scholars who examine the same situation in a wider context have a fuller sense of pattern, look at wider ranges of cause and effect, and hence see from different focal lengths. That means that they take quite different views (for which the equally ugly anthropological neologism *etic* is usually reserved).

Yet both the people and the social scientist *should* ask some specific questions about what actually changed. Were the pressures brought on by change endured a month, a year, or ten years? Is it possible to go back to the way things were before those changes occurred? Temporary changes may lead to grave discomfort in spite of the fact that they are temporary. They are not, however, permanent. The basic criteria for distinguishing the two are whether people actually can go back to the earlier situation, and whether they want to go back.

WHAT HAS CHANGED? A QUESTIONNAIRE

To determine just what has actually changed, we must reduce our questions to address the absolute fundamentals of human living. They may seem totally simplistic, but it is at this basic level that people experience culture change.

1. What do we now eat?

- Do I get my food from different sources than I did before?
- Have new food products been added or old ones disappeared? New drinks? Has alcohol consumption changed?
- Are old ways and new ways of getting food intermixed?

–What do I have to do to make a living now that I did not do before? Can I in fact change what it is I have to do?

–What advantages or disadvantages do I experience because of changes in ways of getting food?

2. What do we now wear? How do we get clothes? Has that changed?

3. What do I now have to do to get what my family and I need to live?

- Do I (or others) have to use new tools that I formerly did not have to use?
- Did my daily round of activities change? If so, were the changes to my disadvantage? How?
- What change has occurred in the actions required to provide food, clothing, and shelter?
- Did my source of income change? What is my job history? What do I have to do now to get food and other necessities that I didn't do before? What has that change cost me in time, in comfort, in security?
- Compared to other people, am I adequately recompensed for what I do?
- Has the division of labor between men and women changed? Between old and young?

- Are some people worse off and some better off than formerly? Who are they? Where do I fit in, and what has happened to my capacity to participate in social events and to predict the results of my actions?

4. Whose place is this? This question breaks down into two subordinate questions:

- First, whose *space* is this? What are my rights in it? With whom do I share those rights?
- Second, whose *land* is this? What are my rights in it? This point is far too often seen as merely a matter of "ownership" of land, as the idea of ownership is outlined in American or European law and culture. It is *far* more complex than that, dealing as it does with natural products of the land and sea.
- What rights have I lost and what have I gained? What can I do now that I couldn't do before? What could I do before that I can't do now? What can I do that others can't? What can they do that I can't?

5. Whom can I trust?

- Do I depend on different people now than formerly? Did dependable family members change?
- Do I depend on the same people for different things?
- Has there been a change in what my kinsmen and I do for each other?
- Do I interact with different people than I did before? How much time does that take?
- Are there more or fewer strangers? Has my relationship with strangers changed?
- Do other people do their jobs as readily and efficiently as they used to?
- Do I depend more or less on some institution, such as the government, than I did formerly?
- Whom do I choose to spend time with? Has that changed?
- Whom do I have to neglect in order to take care of new people and new concerns?
- Is there more or less racial or ethnic prejudice and conflict—more distrust of strangers—than formerly?

6. Has my community changed?

- Do different people now share their food with me? Do I share my food with different people?
- Has people's behavior changed toward me? Has mine changed toward them?
- Has community solidarity decreased or increased?
- Are there more or fewer factions within the community?

7. Who's in charge here?

- Who tells me what I have to do? Has that changed?
- Has the organization of authority changed? Do I still know where I stand with regard to local government? To other people?
- Has leadership changed?
- Have my legal rights changed significantly?
- Has my freedom of movement—migration, visiting, going where I please—changed?

8. Whom do we marry?

- Has the range from which spouses can be chosen increased or decreased?
- Have attitudes toward sex, either marital or nonmarital, changed?
- What are the attitudes toward out-group marriage?

9. Who educates our children?

- Are they taught what I want them to be taught? Is that an advantage for them or just some prejudices of mine?
- What impact does this education have on family and community?
- Does education distance children from the culture of their parents? Is it worth it? Why?

10. Who takes care of my health and my family's health?
11. What—and whom—can I believe?

- Was my religious life affected? Was the influence of the religion increased or decreased? If so, how? Is there serious conflict among the various branches or sects? Has that influenced social life? Has it grown or been reduced?

- Has my basic outlook on the nature of the world changed?

–Did I believe anything earlier that it is no longer possible or sensible to believe?

–What is my outlook about being part of the global community?

–What are human rights? Have they changed?

12. What do I do for fun?
13. Finally, who am I?

- Have I had to change my view of myself, my identity? That is, am I the same person I was before? If not, what's different? Who was I before? Who am I now? Which is better? Why?
- Have my reference groups changed? That is: do I still compare myself and how I am doing with the same people and how they are doing?

This is only a smattering of the basic questions that have to be answered if we are to understand what has in fact changed, and how the changes have affected people. Every person necessarily expresses himself or herself in terms of some of the culture accessible to that person. When the culture changes, the experience changes and hence the view of oneself and other has changed with it.

The point is that some changes are part of the painless growth and development which every culture undergoes at a faster or slower rate. But some others are not. The facts of what changed are subtle and complex. The fact that the comparative literature on the subject is immense does not guarantee that we know very much about it.

Chapter 9

Innovations and Cultural Cusps

C ulture changes by the same processes that make it work. The processes are so simple that people are likely to assume that they are just common sense.[1]

If a cultural tradition provides people with an efficient, predictable, and pleasant adaptation to their environment, the changes they make in it may be almost imperceptible. Yet people everywhere have new ideas, and many of them create new ways to do things in a mode of play. A few of those new ways may be taken up by other people. Eventually, thus, cultural traditions accommodate small changes.

INNOVATION

Getting new ideas and new things into cultural processes and getting old ones out is an essential measure of how culture works. It is easiest to see in repeating cycles. The simplest repeating cycle is made up of two processes (verbs) and two states of the system (nouns). Michael Thompson cites a simple biological cycle: a hen lays an egg, which hatches into a chicken, which lays an egg, which . . . and so on to infinity. In this all-but-flippant

FIGURE 9–1a

Cycling Event Chain with Emphasis on Morphological Elements

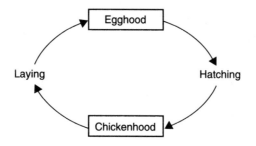

illustration, Thompson calls one morphological state in a cycling chain "chickenhood" and the other "egghood," as shown in Figure 9–1a.

Focusing on the morphological states requires two elements: something has to happen (the verbs) to the morphological entities (the nouns). But if we alter the emphasis by focusing on the predicates—the processes of laying and hatching instead of the morphological units of chicken and egg, shown in Figure 9–1b, we need only one element: the process. Chickenhood and egghood can be seen to be mere temporary morphological states in the flow of the more inclusive process.

Almost as an afterthought, Thompson notes that some aspects of evolution can be explained with the same model that explains the laying and hatching processes. We have only to make room for an input of genetic gain and an output of genetic loss. Figure 9–2 shows how it looks.

FIGURE 9–1b

Cycling Event Chain with Emphasis on Dynamic Processes

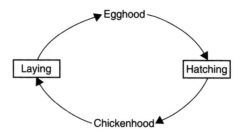

FIGURE 9–2

Fundamentals of Evolution

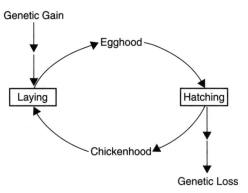

Cultural evolution, arising from social action carried out by individual actors in a medium of culture, can be looked at with the same diagram—Figure 9–3. It now reads: a culture (the bottommost box in Figure 9–3) provides stimulus, in a complex environment, to the acceptor systems of many persons. But stimulus from outside the system, here called "innovation," may also provide immense pressures. Dissatisfaction or creativity may lead people to try to "make things better," or at least different. The combined information—some arriving at the person's acceptor/comparator from the traditional culture and other coming in as innovation—goes through the individual person's filter or monitor, as in Figure 2–2 on page 16. As a result, part of the traditional culture and some or all of the innovation, (a + b) in Figure 9–3, leads to the next action.

That next action, which involves a combination of part (but perhaps not all) of the culture from the last cycle *plus* some (or even all) of the innovation—*that* next action has to be dealt with by other people. The new combinations may be deemed wrong or inadequate by the other actors who participate in the chain, as illustrated for two persons—there can be more—in the social relations of Figure 5–1 on page 52.

Cultural gain can occur only at the level of acceptance of innovation by many persons. In large-scale, complex cultural traditions like our own, social complication may be introduced because some people accept an innovation and others don't. Twelve-tone

FIGURE 9–3

The Basics of Cultural Evolution

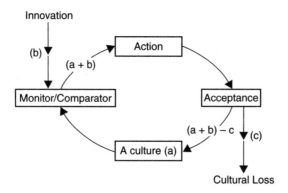

music, for example, was accepted by many composers, but little of it has ever been accepted by the concert-going public. With acceptance, the new trait either becomes part of the general cultural tradition or else new social boundaries spring up within the culture between those who accept it and those who don't.

Whatever action is accepted (whether it got into the cycle as part of the culture or as innovation) now *becomes* traditional as the cycle goes around again. That is to say, the mixture of tradition and innovation becomes the new tradition—obvious until we think about the implications. In these new forms, the information is again assessed by many individual monitors the next time around.

The process shown in Figure 9–3 resembles the market mechanism in that it is the sum of individual choices and interactional pressures. Some of it is dropped (c), some rearranged ([a + b] – c). The point is that the resultant information feeds back through acceptance and may alter the traditional culture and its processes.

Innovation thus follows a pattern very like rubbish theory. Most innovations pass into a sort of limbo and disappear—some merely drop out of sight, but others are actually destroyed. That is, they disappear as "cultural loss" as in Figure 9–3. It is the same process that made those woven pictures called Stevensgraphs disappear—but a few were resurrected. Most Tiv ancestors disappear—but a few become nodes in the Tiv political genealogies. Only a few innovations are accepted—and they may soon be altered by new innovations as the process continues.

———————

Anthropologists have long cited invention and diffusion as the major sources of culture change. We will review both briefly, then go on, in the next chapter, to add other sources of change such as catastrophe, disaster, and recontexting.

Invention. Some people, in some cultures, make inventions—if they get fed up and decide that there must be a better way to do whatever jobs they are faced with, if the physical environment to which they must react changes, or if their social groups grow to the point where the principles that worked in small-scale societies no longer work in large-scale societies. To take an analogy, if the human body were twice as big as it is, it would collapse of its own weight. Something like that happens to cultural traditions—when the society gets big enough, the old system of cultural maintenance will not support its weight. New modes of organization and human expression have to be found.

Cultural attitudes toward innovation vary. Some traditions—especially those with an active market system—reward successful inventions. Other traditions—and some people in all situations—brand any innovation as evil or heresy. Japan in the years before the Meiji Restoration is a vivid example—largely unaware, of course, that their very acts of resisting outside influence led to immense changes in their culture.

One culture change may lead to other changes. Indeed, chains of change may be formed, though that point is difficult to establish without extensive cross-cultural studies made with historical data—studies that have not, as far as I know, been undertaken. However, take an example: at the beginning of the Industrial Revolution in England, weaving machinery was invented to bring down the price of cloth, which had "always" been scarce and expensive. Soon the machines were able to weave much faster than thread could be made. Thereupon the need for spinning machines was felt—and a spinning machine was invented to replace hand-operated spinning wheels. The new spinning and weaving machines meant that the bottleneck now moved back to getting the seeds out of cotton so that the new spinning machines could turn it into thread at their full capacity. By the time the cotton gin was invented to get the seeds out, the original weaving machine had itself become inadequate. New improvements were then made in the weaving machines. In these processes, and within a comparatively few years, a whole textile industry was created. Cloth became inexpensive.

Cheap cloth led to vast change in all parts of the culture. People dressed differently—and their health was affected. They slept differently because bed linens became widely available. They draped their houses differently. All of these things had an impact not only on trade but on family life itself.

In the same way, the steel industry and the automobile industry grew up together. New inventions led to new needs for further inventions. Soon the petroleum industry followed, as the need for a cheap fuel to run automobiles increased. Then came paved roads. Then the Western world's courtship pattern changed as a result of the automobile and all the industries that service it.

The computer industry has more recently launched into a similar development that has not yet reached a plateau. The early personal computers were slow—and the technical goal was to speed up the computer, at least to the point where its users were never aware of waiting for an answer. Computers supplanted word processors, which had supplanted typewriters and carbon paper (which had themselves improved the speed and accuracy of communication and had, once for all, begun the process of breaking down barriers against women as office workers). The victory of desktop computers led to a new industry called the software industry, which in turn demanded new hardware.

Such chains of events have forever altered the way business is done. Computers have made the banking system completely over, and so have altered the world economy. They have altered manufacturing processes, and hence have had an impact on jobs. Today we cannot imagine how people did anything without computers—and we have to realize that maybe they didn't—that our ideas of "anything" have changed.

Our acceptance of computers, much as it has changed our lives, has not been upsetting or painful. The fact that some people won't use computers doesn't mean that they haven't accepted computers, only that some significant proportion of people have to adopt a change in order to make it a part of everybody's new tradition.

The computer age has also had an immense impact on education. Not only did traditional students come to learn computer skills, but computers changed the position of mathematics in the total curriculum. They further changed the position of women by banishing the prejudice that using a keyboard was woman's work. Most important, the uneducated—and even the educated who are not computer literate—have been pushed to the sidelines of the unemployed, perhaps to the point of being unemployable. "Keeping up" with computers means that both universities and company training programs have to adapt to them continually, and the position of formal education in our lives is no longer confined to our early years but has become a lifetime pursuit.

The changes that the computer has wrought in society are almost unimaginable, even though many of us have lived through those changes from their inception—indeed, I myself once shook hands with John von Neumann. We badly need more detailed comparative studies of the patterns of flow in culture change.

Social inventions are at least as powerful as technological inventions in transforming the way we live. Consider these:

The clan was an invention for turning some, but not all, kinship relationships to totally new purposes. The maximum size of a manageable society could, as a result, grow from several hundred to several hundred thousand members.

The state was an invention for creating a hierarchy of roles in which power could be lodged, independent of specific individuals. Modern political organization—and its impact on all other dimensions of culture—was the result.

The publicly-owned corporation was an invention for financing large undertakings when nobody else (neither state nor church) had the resources or the will to undertake them. The idea of shareholding companies is very old, but the idea of turning such a company into a legal person that can exist through time, and can undertake many different ventures instead of a single one, developed in Holland, France, and England in the 1500s and 1600s.

Anglo-America was colonized after the victory of the corporation; Latin America was colonized before. The difference is still with us.

The production line (a social invention) was as important as the reaper. It altered the work lives of vast numbers of people almost out of recognition. The corporation was as important an invention as the steam engine. Democracy was as important an invention as the plow.

Limits to Invention. We have not learned to free social inventions from fear of change. The need for new social inventions has never been more urgent than it is today. We desperately need new social institutions that can amass enough capital to clean up the environment and deal with problems of poverty. Although corporations and national governments have begun the process, it remains to be seen whether they can be successful.

We also need new social devices for educating people of all ages in a situation in which traditional educational institutions no longer work.

But inventing new social tools and institutions—and getting them accepted—is far more difficult than inventing new technological tools. The reason is simple: new technical tools demand that we first change our work patterns—the social and moral changes follow along, almost beneath our awareness. New social inventions, however, require that we change our *moralities*, after which other changes may or may not follow. Unlike computers, social inventions cannot accommodate a class of nonusers. As a result, any person who tries to invent and disseminate social innovations is considered dangerous. Such people undermine the moralities that we value; even when those moralities are destructive, we move to protect them.

Furthermore, nobody has yet figured out how to copyright or patent new social institutions—and hence how to get rich off them. Governments may throw money at "problems," but the purpose is seldom actually to change the social situation that created the problems. Their efforts seldom lead to new kinds of social institutions designed to alter the conditions that led to the problems in the first place. The Kerner Commission Report[2]—which did suggest new ways to deal with racism in the United States—was an exception. It is still relevant—and still languishes unheeded.

At one level, this kind of conservatism is a virtue, because new social systems may end up as revolutions or else waste decades before they prove to be unworkable.

Thus, people almost invariably try to solve problems by using the social arrangements they already know, with the result that social change sneaks up on them. We have not yet learned to test the feasibility of social inventions without putting the whole society through a trying period that may end in failure. If social scientists can figure out how to do that, their enterprise will have risen to a new plane.

Inventiveness, whether technological or social, is limited by cultural preconditions. An invention is of no immediate value if its necessary preconditions are not present. Leonardo da Vinci invented the airplane in about 1500 A.D., but because the internal combustion engine had not been invented, and for many other such reasons, it could not be built.

Bathroom inventions show how closely acceptance of innovations are tied to culturally derived ideas like cleanliness and privacy. The Romans saw a bath as a public event and maintained huge public baths. Victorians saw a bathroom as no more than a place, very privately, to get clean. American hot tubs are somewhere in the middle.

Inventions of new types of household or office furniture are closely associated with cultural ideas of comfort (which changed radically in Europe and America in the 1700s and again in the 1900s) as well as being about efficiency and privacy, intimacy and social relationships.

The public reception of an invention is, to repeat, more determinative of future culture than is its creation. Thousands of inventions are made each month, many of them even patented. If the public is not interested, such inventions disappear—our attics are full of patents for inventions that never caught on. Some of these rejected inventions may be reinvented once the preconditions are right—that is, once there is a public readiness to accept the other changes that the new invention requires. I know a man who invented an ingenious engine based on the Möbius strip—a highly fuel-efficient engine that could be made to burn with little emission. But he discovered that, except for his method of sealing, it had been patented in the 1890s. His reinvention was useless in today's America because he could not patent it, and hence nobody could make any money from manufacturing it. The fact that it is more efficient and cleaner than the piston engine is not, in our system, considered adequate reason for experimenting with switching over to a new kind of engine.

Acceptance of social inventions is far more complex. It depends in large part on whether or not people are uncomfortable enough with their present way of doing things that they are willing to change their habit patterns—that is (in terms of Figure 2–2), to change their responses. Yet such social inventions as the encounter group were accepted in the early 1960s, and support groups soon became common.

Diffusion. A second way to get new culture is to borrow ideas, technology, and social arrangements. That process has traditionally been called diffusion. Diffusion is very like recontexting, but the size and range of the social group involved is larger, or at least contains greater cultural variety. Recontexting is done within a cultural tradition; diffusion is the same thing among cultural traditions. Again, the definition of cultural tradition is the crucial point—and that is done primarily by anthropologists who may, in optimal circumstances, be reporting what people on the ground say about a situation.

Tools can be borrowed and copied from the cultural tradition next door—or from people next door who have opted for a lifestyle different from ours. Tools and ideas can, indeed, be taken over from one's enemies. The details of *Panzer* attacks and the tune of "Lili Marlene" crossed sides in World War II. Meanings too can be learned from more or less distant neighbors. Tools may be put to different uses in a new context; ideas that first had one meaning in one context may, after they are borrowed, turn into ideas that are utterly different from anything heretofore known.

Some inventions or borrowings, once made and accepted, spread rapidly. The idea of agriculture, for example, was invented several times, in several parts of the world. It diffused quickly from those points. The use of new food crops also spreads rapidly. Beef, for example, came from the Old World to the New very soon after the Spanish invasion. Potatoes went from the New World to the Old. Maize, a New World crop, became one of the staple foods of Africa within a very short period. The idea of the water-wheel to turn gears, and then of the *noria*, a water-wheel with buckets to raise water from low to higher levels, spread rapidly. So did the windmill.

In the late 1800s and the early 1900s, anthropologists were still arguing heatedly about whether *any* invention could be made more than once. Could the same improvement be invented many times or is every invention diffused from one original source? Today we know that the same inventions are often made in many places—and also that the diffusion of both ideas and technology takes place not only all the time but in a regular order. Each situation offers cultural choices—but once a choice is made, a new situation has arisen, and with it a new set of choices.

As with inventions, the acceptance of a diffused idea or item is the vital point. Many peoples know about superior technologies or practices of their neighbors, yet do not choose to use them—to do so would create unacceptable changes in other parts of their own culture and would lead them to have to change their own habit patterns.

CULTURAL CUSPS

Over time, small changes stack up. Two things can happen—two kinds of cusp. One is historical or evolutionary; the other is perceptual.

If many small changes lead to conditions that make it impossible to return to an earlier adjustment, an evolutionary change has occurred—cultural evolution is determined far less by what is added than by what is lost.

Perceptual change is more subtle but no less important. Although some people obviously realize, at some level, that change is occurring, they may not make a specific point of it or even adjust their activities to it. People probably won't change their lives bit by bit, in sync with the changes around them. Rather, they do their changing in spurts, as they realize that something is wrong that used to be right. When the cumulative change becomes massive enough, people realize—perhaps suddenly—that their situation has become very different and that old ways are gone. Old ways seem to be irrelevant—they may even be unintelligible. Almost never do people understand the processes by which that difference has been brought about. They are likely, rather, to ascribe the newly realized difference to a specific event.

Here I am calling the first kind of change evolutionary change. The second can be called paradigm change. The criterion for the first is that you cannot go back to earlier cultural adjustments; the criterion for the second is that people amalgamate all the changes into a few big events—sometimes a single event—and see a paradigm shift. Seldom do they try to understand the process. Figure 9–4 shows how paradigm changes work.

Cultural Evolution. The idea of evolution is an ancient one— Greek philosophers thought about it; Latin poets wrote about it. It is a simple idea: every social or technological situation allows certain possible choices, and hence changes. Forces always gather both to encourage and to prevent changes. However, if and when those forces of conservatism are overcome and a change actually occurs, the results of the change alter the possibilities. Options that were possible earlier may no longer be available; new options are opened up for the first time.

The ideas of cultural evolution were, when they were first mooted, not in the least threatening to anybody—and by and large they still are not. However, a huge controversy erupted when the old idea of evolution was recontexted into biology, where it contradicted entrenched religious dogma. The idea of biological evolution forced a new look at accepted answers to eternal questions. Even in the present day, some people still refuse to accept the idea of evolution applied to biology even though those same people do not question the idea when it is applied to culture.

Evolution requires an input of new information into a genetic or cultural pool. Just as important, it requires a way for the sys-

FIGURE 9–4

The Course of Incremental Culture Change

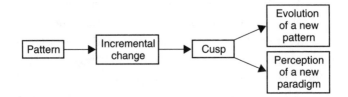

tem to get rid of genetic information or cultural traditions. The processes by which evolution proceeds are of course the very processes by which culture change occurs—with one additional factor. An evolutionary step is defined by a stage at which the choices have changed so much that it is impossible to go back to the way things were before the process began. There is no way that the world's people today could go back to peasant farming—in the first place, there are too many of us for that world to support by that means. But even if 90 percent (say) of our population were liquidated, the survivors would *know* too much. The ideas in our heads would soon get us beyond peasant farming.

Cultural evolution ultimately depends on the type and rate of culture loss. If enough improvements in the efficiency and rewards of culture are made, it becomes unthinkable that people would try to live without them. If, as a result of some catastrophe, the world were to lose agriculture, the ideas of agriculture would be in the heads of any survivors and they would manage to reconstruct it. It is true that any details that were not in the heads of the particular survivors would have to be either forgone or reinvented, but enough is in their heads that agriculture could soon be reestablished. The same is true of something as simple as money: once we understand the way the several functions of money fit together, its simplifying force means that no one would be able to go back to the days before money was invented. Both money and agriculture are simplifying ideas that are essential in large-scale societies. They will be retained unless they are replaced with more efficient means of doing what they do. If we were to lose computers, total ruin would befall the global society that has so recently emerged. Although it is too early to tell for sure, we could probably not go back to the smaller national forms of economy and polity that preceded the computer. If the right people survive, they could reinvent computers—but if all the hackers are gone, then true disaster has struck.

Paradigm Shifts. An unusual event sometimes makes everyone suddenly aware of all the changes that have in fact occurred. It creates a point-of-before-it-and-after-it. Although people may be aware of some cultural changes while they are occurring, they adapt to others without noticing. Then, when some event occurs that makes them suddenly aware of the changes, that event becomes a cusp in the story, one that people tell, write about, and remember. The shift is remarkably similar to a paradigm shift in the history of science.

Disasters can readily be experienced as cusps that lead to paradigm shifts. A vivid example is that just after World War II the British constantly told one another, "things are different since the war." The war may not have been primarily responsible for many of the changes that were taking place, but because it was the dominating event of the period, the war became the cusp. Warfare as an agent of change is discussed in the next chapter.

If the various small changes that mesh on the cusp are inconsistent among themselves (or if they deny human biological requirements), the result may be disaster. The demise of Soviet communism is an example of a cultural system that slowly destroyed itself, but the experience of that process of destruction was far more sudden than the process itself.

Cultural cusps happen closer together as complexity grows and as people have more choices to make. The archaeological eras of the Stone Age, Bronze Age, and Iron Age were long periods—but each one was shorter than the last. Changes proceeded so slowly that they were probably not noticeable to the people living through them. Those people's minds—like everybody else's—were necessarily focused on getting along from day to day. But the paradigm shifts were almost surely experienced (by different peoples at different times, to be sure) as sudden, and perhaps painful.

As culture becomes more complex—indeed, as there come to be more and more different manifestations of it—the choices open to people become more numerous. As different people make different choices, different cultural traditions come to be housed, as it were, in the same geographical space. New ways of dealing with the resulting social differentiation are required.

Technological improvements can of course lead to culture cusps. For example, in several parts of the world a strong desire to trade and to explore new lands led to improvements in sailing ships and navigational instruments. In Europe after the fourteenth century such technological improvements led to what Euro-Americans chauvinistically call the voyages of discovery. Those Europeans eventually created global mercantile empires— a cusp that changed the entire world.

With every cultural cusp, whole ranges of peoples' expectations are transformed. The cycles of activity that fill their daily lives are vastly different from those of their ancestors. The trajectories of the social relations and activities that people live by are altered.

Contemporary civilization would seem right now to be in the throes of a gigantic cultural cusp. Most of us can look back through our lives and realize that we have lived through such a cusp—perhaps several. Today we are keenly aware of living on a cusp created by efficient and fast global communication. We can't quite fathom what the events will be that will present us with new social and cultural paradigms, more or less as a *fait accompli*. Our needs for resources and excitement, among other things, are driving us to explore the bottom of the sea and are thrusting us into space. The new technologies, discoveries, and opportunities that result from space exploration are likely to induce social changes as great as those produced by the agricultural or industrial revolutions.

Culture cusps cannot be planned. They come about because of invention and the diffusion and gradual acceptance of new ways. As the changes accumulate, people can no longer ignore the realization that "everything is different."

To sum up, culture *change* occurs all the time. Culture *cusps* occur when the changes more or less suddenly become overwhelming— what seem to be totally new patterns appear. Cultural *evolution* occurs whenever sufficient new culture is taken up and old culture is lost so that we cannot go back to earlier ways. New cultural *paradigms* occur when people realize that the change is in fact already made and that new ways of looking at things have triumphed.

Understanding the flow and ebb of culture and of its many parts is, in a sense, counterintuitive. Yet we all know that today is not quite like yesterday, and tomorrow will be different from today. The differences may seem trivial and irrelevant—until we run into the paradigm shifts that make us realize that we have changed our ways, or until cultural evolution makes it impossible for us to go back to yesterday.

Chapter 10

Disasters and Cultural Traps

D isasters lead to culture change in a way very different from the collective adjustments that mount up into a cusp. Disasters smash everything, leaving the survivors to adjust, sometimes without adequate tools and often without meanings.

But thinking about disasters—anthropologically or any other way—is a minefield. Finding our way through that minefield depends on the particular distinctions we make. First of all, it is fruitful for us to distinguish disasters that follow dislocations in the physical world from biological disasters, then both from social disasters. Some social disasters strike from outside a cultural system; they must be distinguished from the cultural traps that are set, and sometimes sprung, within the system. We must then distinguish both traps and external disasters from cultural dissonance, which may accompany both and of which there are at least two types: the dissonance between the cultures of neighbors who live within a single social space, and the dissonance that results when culture in the head is out of sync with culture in the environment.

This chapter is about disasters that strike from the outside, like earthquakes and conquests; it also contains a preliminary discussion of social traps. The next chapter is about dissonances that occur when two or more cultural systems in the same social space are at loggerheads and nobody understands which one to follow or how to get them together.

Disaster as a term is treacherous mainly because there are many kinds of disasters and each works in its own way. Even to define *disaster* is difficult because so many criteria can be considered. All words that are used as technical terms need to be carefully controlled, but the difficulty is particularly great when we talk about disasters.

An earthquake is not a disaster from a geological point of view. The disaster arises when the earthquake disrupts human action chains. Because evaluation and interpretation are required to turn a natural or social event into "a disaster," disasters always have a cultural referent. Although anything that is antisurvival or antiadaptability will readily be conceded as disastrous by everybody, some cultural traditions add more referents. The greater the human adjustment required, the worse the disaster.

The English language, and probably most others, is rich in "disaster" terms: *calamity, catastrophe, cataclysm, emergency, accident*, even *tragedy*. Each has a slightly different emphasis. *The American Heritage Dictionary* compares and contrasts

- *disaster*, which implies immense destruction, hardship and loss of life,
- *calamity*, which stresses grief and sense of loss,
- *catastrophe*, which stresses a tragic final outcome,
- *cataclysm*, which is a violent upheaval that brings about a fundamental change.

These words also carry a heavy emotional overload that, unless it is recognized, interferes with their use as technical terms for the simple reason that their emotional aura, either conscious or unconscious, colors people's attitudes and hence the meaning that they give them. There are other problems—assignment of blame not the least among them. In some societies, hurricanes or earthquakes can be blamed on witches; in many, revolutions can be blamed on individual thinkers like Marx; in our own, industrial disasters can be blamed on corporations that exist to produce the products necessary to run our culture. Those industrial disasters may result from faulty processes, or human error—and, of course, we may be suspicious of the motives of the corporate officers.

In using words such as those in the list, we must analyze carefully not only how we are using them but *why* we are using them. It is also necessary to remember that when we classify disasters, the categories cannot be watertight: some events overlap the categories, no matter how carefully we build them.

With such warnings in mind, we can differentiate among physical disasters, biological disasters, and cultural (here including social) disasters—the three major realms of reality. Of each kind, we must inquire about the several defining characteristics:

1.   What caused the disaster? Another way of putting much the same question is: What kind of event chains led to the disaster or were interrupted by the disaster?

2.   What is the purpose of the person making the classification? Sociologist Kai Erikson, for example, classifies disasters into natural and technological.[1] For the problems he is examining—the psychological and social impact of modern-day industrial disasters that end up in the courts—that is a sufficient categorization. However, we dare not assume that his (or any other) classification is adequate when we are concerned with different problems—certainly not all imaginable, or even all documentable disasters fall into one of those two categories.

3.   What specific human activities have been made difficult or impossible by the event classified as a disaster?

4.   What cultural items and traditions inform recovery efforts? In physical disasters like earthquakes or floods, some buildings or other cultural manifestations may be reduced to ruin or swept away, but most parts of the culture that were there before the disaster survive. The culture of helpers like the Red Cross may be added, but they too may have been part of the pre-disaster culture. On the other hand, in sociocultural disaster such as conquest, whole new realms of culture may have been added to the context of recovery.

DISASTER CATEGORIES

Physical Disasters. Under physical disasters we can cite earthquakes, volcanic eruptions, hurricanes, and floods. They alter the environments where people live and must adapt to survive. They may cause death, destruction of homesites, or destruction of the means of subsistence. If they kill large numbers of people, or if settlements must be moved, or if the juxtaposition of people within the settlement is affected, such catastrophes have important social fallout.

Physical disasters do not—in themselves, they cannot—create *cultural* conflict. People may suffer depression because of the immense loss they have experienced. They will almost surely seek better ways to do things, which may spur incremental change. New disagreements may erupt among members of the community about how to run a new order that they believe has been forced on them. But physical disasters do not—cannot—lead to cultural dissonance (an idea to be discussed in the next chapter) as social disasters do.

Physical disasters are invariably followed by a struggle to reestablish "normal" life. Any inclinations to change the culture following a disaster are attempts to make things either safer or otherwise better than they were before the disaster. California engineers, after each major earthquake, study the damage specifically so they can improve their knowledge of the causes of structural collapse; that knowledge is soon put into architectural practice and, indeed, into the building codes. The major thrust for most citizens, however, is to get life back to normal. New factions may indeed form as people attempt to get back to normal; the factionalism may be destructive. Some people may try to use the catastrophic situation to improve their own power positions. It may also be true that the social structure cannot be, after the adjustment to the disaster, precisely the same as it was before. Distinguishing the disaster itself from incremental change and growth in the processes of facing the results of the disaster is difficult, and it may even be wrongheaded because they are parts of a single process.

Two sudden physical disasters in Alaska offer vivid examples. On June 6, 1912, Mount Katmai on the Alaska Peninsula blew up after having been quiet for many centuries. A series of violent explosions threw six cubic miles of debris into the air, weighing more than 33 billion tons. The geologist who wrote the generally accepted analysis of this explosion noted that the eruption was as if Manhattan Island had blown up with no survivors. The sound could have been heard in Chicago; acid rain in Toronto would have raised blisters on the Torontoneans' skin; and a foot of ash would have fallen on Philadelphia.[2] The ash from the Mount Katmai eruption drifted toward the east and southeast—more than 30,000 square miles of sea and land were covered as much as a foot deep with it, creating devastation on the land from which it was to take many years to recover. At sea, the ash killed fish and mammals. The city of Kodiak, 100 miles away, was in the direct line of the clouds of dust and ash. It was plunged into total darkness—much deeper darkness than the darkness of night—for 60 hours. Some areas of the city were under several feet of volcanic ash.

On Kodiak Island, the villages of Old Harbor, Kaguyak, Afognak, and Ouzinkie suffered greatly. People from these villages were evacuated to Anchorage, where they were put into shelters operated by the Red Cross. New villages were built, others were moved. The city of Kodiak was rebuilt. Although I can find no records of the specific social changes wrought by the eruption, we know that with the relocations the relative positions of persons and of communities were changed, and that that is always an indicator of cultural change. Almost surely there were significant changes in the power structures of the community members. Almost surely their cultural tool kits were modernized in the process of being replaced.

Then, on March 27, 1964, an earthquake measuring from 8.3 to 8.7 on the Richter scale—"one of the greatest recorded earthquakes of all time"[3]—destroyed much of Anchorage and all other human structures in the area of Cook Inlet and Prince William Sound. The quake and the tsunamis that followed it devastated Valdez, Whittier, Seward, Kodiak, and Homer. Cordova and Seldovia were both seriously affected—and Cordova was already suffering the effects of a fire that had wiped out three quarters of its business district. As the result of the quake, Cordova was lifted six to seven feet up, which made its tides lower, its harbor shallower, and put its canneries far above the waterline. Thirty-one persons died in Valdez; the town had to be completely relocated, four miles from its original site. Its entire waterfront burned for two weeks after an oil-tank farm caught fire. Descriptions of "miles of floating oil and wreckage" on Prince William Sound appeared in the press at the time.

The intertidal zone of Prince William Sound was permanently altered; at least 36 percent of the clams were destroyed. In some areas the land was uplifted as much as 50 feet. Tsunamis caused untold damage to the freshwater lakes near the shore. Fires in oil-storage-tank farms released gasoline—Cook Inlet was covered with a thin coat of gasoline for several days.

Three Native Alaskan villages were devastated; five others suffered great damage. Chenega, on an island in Prince William Sound, was totally destroyed. One third of its residents—twenty-three out of seventy-six—were lost. The survivors were flown to Cordova, where they were cared for in the Cordova Community Baptist Church. The survivors chose not to try to rebuild their village, but rather to live in Tatitlek. Not until twenty years later, in 1983, did some of them (together with a few other people) build a new village—Chenega Bay—near the site of the one that had been destroyed.

Physical disasters may cause great suffering but they do not much alter cultural traditions. New challenges to the people who suffer such disasters may at first appear overwhelming, but nobody has to change his or her mind about the nature of human society, human endeavor, or how things should be done. The response to the challenge to improve the cultural situation—to make things "better" than they were—is likely to create as much change as the physical disaster itself.

Biological Disasters. Biological disasters resemble physical disasters in many ways. The most obvious biological disasters arise from epidemics of disease. Again, epidemics occur from perfectly normal biological processes. Epidemics, however, are not merely biological—human behavior is usually involved in spreading the disease, in reacting to it and treating it, and in recovering from it. Because all such activities are culture laden, a cultural dimension is integral to them. Disease epidemics in recent centuries (and probably always) have been handmaidens of conquest, which spreads the diseases themselves and which creates new settlement patterns and demographic conditions that exacerbate them.

Epidemic disease is one of the bleakest kinds of disaster—its results can totally alter social and cultural adjustments. When the disaster has passed, some sort of cultural tradition must be assembled by whoever survives from whatever cultural elements have survived. Demographically the society may be precipitously reduced in numbers; economically the bases of its security may have been totally wiped out as new technological processes and new divisions of labor realign people's tasks. Estimates about the proportion of the Native American population who were killed by European diseases after Europeans first erupted into their midst runs as high as 95 percent, but that figure is probably too high; we will never, obviously, have precise figures. The same can be said of the peoples of the Pacific Islands—it was even postulated at one time that the diseases brought to those islands by European conquerors so decimated the peoples there that they might not survive at all.

Social Disasters. Social disasters seem to be more crippling even than physical or biological disasters precisely because they so insidiously undermine the common cultural understandings in people's heads. Physical disasters can and do disrupt that part of culture that lies in the external world and hence lead to what will be called *dissonance* in the next chapter. But they do not—by themselves, they cannot—directly affect the culture in people's heads. They may, of course, contribute to the kind of malaise in which people abandon hope—and their culture with it. Both biological disasters and physical disasters, when they impact culture, do it in that way.

The misuse or failure of complex technology can sometimes lead to a disaster that may be regarded as cultural in origin, but with results similar to those of physical disaster because they change only the culture of the external world. Chernobyl and Bhopal are examples. Most disasters that result from technological failure are, like the automobile accident rate, integral aspects of the cultural tradition no matter how much we deplore them. Fail-safe becomes a cultural goal.

Social disasters arise in two ways. First, an ongoing social process leads to unexpected and unwanted disastrous outcomes; I will call these *cultural traps*, although "cultural implosion" is also an apt description. Second, ongoing social processes can be knocked off course by social events such as conquest and colonization that come from totally outside the ongoing processes. We can call them *calamities*. (It's a pity that the word "extraplosion" hasn't yet been coined.) We will look at both.

Cultural traditions can become a cultural trap. The ancient Greeks, having founded the city-state, got mired in it. Turmoil within, and struggles between, city-states created some of the factors that ultimately led to cultural collapse. The Greeks could not figure out how to get out of the bind—indeed, they seem not even to have known that they were in a bind. The Greeks are still there, but the classical Greek cultural tradition perished.

The Maya suffered a similar predicament: after brilliant achievement, people got stuck in the contradictions of what they had themselves created. The complexities of the Maya religion underlay their political process. The Maya, like the Greeks, could not avoid struggles between city-states. They could not question their religious premises, which intensified those struggles. The descendants of the Maya people are still there, but their ancient cultural tradition is mostly a memory.

This type of social disaster—a culture collapsing of its own weight and internal contradictions—has happened most recently in the Soviet Union. The people are still there. They will do something—and whatever they do may well determine the next stage of our global culture. That collapse in 1989 was experienced by many Soviet people as an unmitigated national disaster.

HOW CULTURAL TRAPS MAKE SOCIAL DISASTERS WORSE

When parts of a cultural tradition get a hold on the human mind in a way that makes it impossible for people to separate culture from the natural (physical and biological) and social dimensions of their situation, their perspective and vision narrow. Whenever people cannot think about either their natural or social worlds without such crippling cultural premises, they are already in a cultural trap.

If the environment, including the social environment, changes in such a way that a cultural tradition is no longer an advantage in dealing with that environment, the tradition's imperatives become the iron teeth of a cultural trap that closes tight, making further adaptation impossible.

Scientific explanation, religious faith, political correctness—in fact, any cultural virtue—may become a cultural trap. A virtue turns into a cultural trap if people slavishly follow some specific formulation of it—if they cannot examine and question the context and results of their virtue. As conditions change, any religious explanations or political convictions that stifle thought and preclude questioning become deadly. When that happens, the very culture that had helped its people solve whatever problems they in fact solved can become a trap that destroys everything their ancestors worked for. Any people who are not willing to reconsider old ideas as they slip into new contexts may be doomed to live in a fatal cultural dead end.

Many people in today's world consider warfare the most virulent of all social disasters. Warfare is difficult to examine in neutral analytical terms because we have to back up and take longer looks at a more inclusive social situation, and also because we have to overcome our tendency to analyze its tactics. We find it hard to learn to stop asking how to win it or how to stop it, and get on with analyzing its processual dimension. Warfare demands two sides (there may, of course, be more). That fact alone may be difficult to achieve—it took decades of adjusting sides, and making people see them as sides, before the American Civil War could take place. The first thing we have to do is to get used to the fact that the two sides are part of an inclusive social-action chain. Some cultural traditions build warfare into their action cycles— indeed, it can even be said with some justification that we ourselves build it in, insofar as we are unable to get beyond our current international questions and find the next ones.

It has even been demonstrated that warfare may be the most important single situation promoting cultural change.[4] Probably all societies exist in two modes: the peaceful and the mobilized.[5] The rates and focuses of incremental change in the two modes can be entirely different. With mobilization, the focus of social institutions is narrowed; inventiveness is centered on weaponry; resistance to new culture—at least the weaponry and defense parts of it—is lowered.

Because anthropologists have spent far less time with the impact of warfare on any society than they have spent on the impact of Western expansion and conquest on small-scale societies and the colonial empires that have resulted, I will say no more about warfare as a disaster or as the sire of cultural change. Few anthropologists have ever been in a position to witness warfare among the peoples they study, but almost every anthropologist studies people who have at some time been impacted by conquest and colonialism.

Externally Caused Calamity. The kind of social disaster that originates outside the system—what we have here called a *calamity*—works very differently from the cultural trap. Conquest and occupation that crush entire political systems and perhaps lead to colonialism have been central to anthropological data and analysis as well as to world history. The experiences of the peoples of the New World, Africa, Oceania, Australia, and Siberia in dealing with the expansion of Europe in the years after 1400 A.D. provide literally thousands of vivid examples. People living in complex states and empires like those of Middle America, India, and West Africa were hit as hard as people who lived in smaller societies.

THE AFTEREFFECTS OF DISASTER

Both physical and social disasters may affect tools and traditional action chains. Both may redistribute people on the ground, with accompanying social and psychological pressures. However, physical disasters in themselves can never introduce new material (that is, tangible) culture and new idea systems that render traditional meanings meaningless. Such cultural discontinuity is the very substance of social disasters. Physical disasters ordinarily disrupt behavior; social disasters not only disrupt behavior, even to the point of destroying whole systems of ideas and values; they may also fuel new systems of thought, thus destroying the old culture even more efficiently. Physical disasters may lead people to necessary creativity, but in no way do they provide readymade alternatives as social disasters sometimes do.

After any disaster, people work at adapting to new situations with their old premises and with the cultural ideas and things that they dragged with them from their predisaster lives. In times of physical (including technological) disaster, underlying cultural premises do not change. Physical disasters are necessarily followed *only* by efforts to mend existing patterns of culture (which may grow by increment in the process) for the simple reason that no other cultural elements that can be recontexted have been introduced into the environment.

After conquest, however, the alien culture thickens the very atmosphere. Efforts, in that atmosphere, to reassert old patterns may well lead to still further disaster. The conquered people must create a new pattern, using not only the shards of their own cultural tradition that they can find among the ruins, but also whatever can be recontexted from the culture of the conquerors. Thus, whenever social disaster damages a cultural pattern, the survivors are faced with a need to use their creative capacities not only to restore order but also to adjust their cultural patterns to new ideas and tools imposed from the outside. A period of uncertainty, and perhaps chaos, accompanies social disaster before any new culture pattern is mature enough to take hold.

Social disasters create cultural change not only by killing off large segments of the population or by altering social efficiencies. Their deadliest impact arises because they render meaningless the ideas of the traditional culture.

Figure 10–1 provides a summary of the distinctions we have made so far. The general topic of cultural change can be divided into change that occurs by increment versus change by disaster. At the second level, distinctions among the physical, biological, and cultural realms are emphasized. Cultural disasters may occur when culture traps are sprung or with the impact of foreign, incompatible cultures.

Some of these ideas can also be expressed as flowcharts, as shown in Figure 10–2, where we see that (A) culture traps take a process deeper and deeper into trouble until collapse occurs, whereas (B) calamities are created when an ongoing process is derailed by impact from outside.

Several principles can be drawn from the above discussion. First of all, disasters call up conscious and purposeful cultural creativity of a sort never required when change takes place by incre-

FIGURE 10–1

Some Distinctions for Analyzing Culture Change

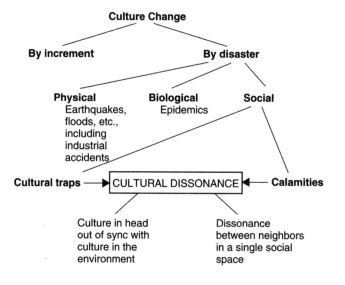

FIGURE 10–2

Cultural Traps and Calamities

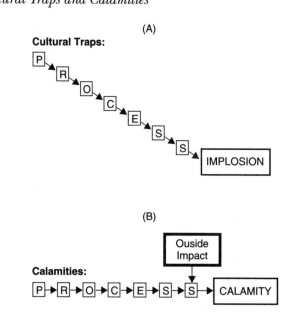

ments. Increments occur from day to day—they come to be realized, but do not require a special effort to make cultural sense out of living in the environment. Disasters, on the other hand, have to be dealt with as emergencies. If the culture for dealing with them is not at hand, it has to be fashioned, and quickly.

Physical disasters and social disasters lead to different processes for creating new cultural tradition. After a physical disaster, the challenge to recreate and improve on the old culture may give rise to change, but such change is not perceived as a threat. However, after a social disaster, former tools and ideas and behavior may have been rendered inadequate by the presence of new ones that may not yet be adequately understood. If that is so, the old order cannot be reestablished. Moreover, some types of social disaster, particularly conquest, add another feature: the available culture—ideas and tools—for creating the new tradition includes elements from both the conquerors and the conquered, in a mixture that may not be understood by anybody.

The major differences between the outcome of physical and social disaster are summarized in Figure 10–3.

In situations of conquest (and especially full-blown colonialism), new cultural constructions may themselves be shattered if the conquerors or the colonial powers shift policies, or if one colonial power is supplanted by another with different cultural ways,

FIGURE 10–3

Effects of Physical and Social Disaster

Physical Disasters	Social Disasters
Cause alteration of the natural environment to which people must adapt	Cause alteration of the social and/or cultural environment to which people must adapt
Do not, in themselves, create social or cultural conflict, but may lead to social disruption that does create conflict	Result from cultural conflict and usually create further conflict
Do not cause cultural dissonance, an idea to be discussed in Chapter 11	Cause cultural dissonance
Are invariably followed by an attempt to reestablish what the affected people regard as normality	Change ideas of cultural normality

as was the case when the Americans bought Alaska from the Russians. New cultural patterns have to be sought every time such a secondary culture-shattering occurs. That can lead to cascades of culture change, each new pattern leading to new problems and to further alterations of pattern.

The experience of living in a colonial situation of this sort gives people the hopeless feeling that nothing works. The cascades of change lead to despair. People lose both the right to run their own lives and the sense of and responsibility for doing so. They can no longer make all their own decisions; they lose faith in themselves, become listless and apathetic—example after example, from many parts of the world, can be cited. The Yaqui people, who now live in Sonora, Mexico, and in Arizona, had to make four major adjustments in three hundred years—to Spanish colonialism, to the kind of societies that Catholic priests established around their missions, to the kind of demands made by the newly independent Mexican government, and to the demands of modernism in both Mexico and the United States. Each time they successfully

FIGURE 10–4

Processes of Continuous New Impact, as in Colonialism

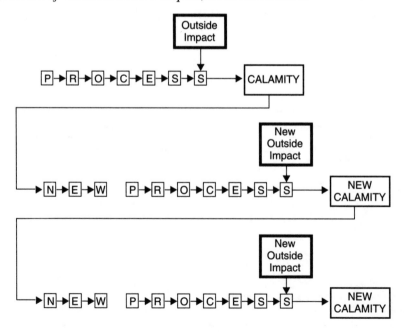

reached new solutions, those solutions were pulled out from under them.[6] Figure 10–4 shows how it works. A Native Alaskan anthropologist has written movingly of the "generations of baggage" that people in that situation take with them—and the way social problems burgeon as more and more disoriented people take refuge in alcohol or drugs.[7]

———————————

To sum up, disasters disturb processes—all processes, be they social, historical, cultural or evolutionary. In formulating the effect of a disaster, one must understand what processes were disrupted, how they were disrupted, whether the disruption was permanent, and whether it altered possible human choices. Disaster is a primary laboratory for studying cultural processes because in times of disaster the processes become overt. People talk about them and generalize the cultural values that will underlie the changes they are forced to make.

Chapter 11

Cultural Dissonance

Meaning is complicated—with time and the flow of events, it can be refined or even completely changed. The circumstances surrounding a significant event determine its initial meaning. As people adjust to it—that is, as they set it into new context—new dimensions of meaning are likely to open up. Then, when the event is recorded, still newer contexts emerge—and meaning must be reconsidered. When the event and its various meanings are analyzed in terms of the premises of political convictions or a scientific discipline, still newer meanings come into play. Historians and ethnographers are keenly aware that finally—and certainly not predictably—readers also bring meanings with them as they read or as they view film.

Anthropologists have developed some skills—not enough, but some—both in controlling the meanings that they translate from a "native" language into English and those they themselves need when they write their ethnographic accounts. Some of them have developed skills to help readers put *their* special meanings on hold while they adjust to the meanings of the people the ethnographer is reporting.

In honing such skills, anthropologists have had to develop a careful awareness of context. They know at first hand, and sometimes painfully, that an act or idea in one cultural tradition (or in one historical period) is likely to be quite different from what appears to be the "same" act in another cultural tradition. In large scale societies, where many complex cultural traditions coexist, context is as cogent for actors as it is for analysts of the situation. What appears at a superficial level to be the same thing may have one meaning in one context, for one set of people, and quite a different meaning in another context, for their neighbors. Such skills for dealing with strangers and strange ways are essential for successful living in complex, multicultural social worlds.

This juxtaposition of events, meaning, and contexts may lead to a problem of dissonance. There are at least two kinds of dissonance. One is what has traditionally been called *cognitive dissonance*,[1] which is dissonance among ideas held by single persons. The other is the kind of dissonance that falls out between persons of different cultural tradition and that can conveniently be called *cultural dissonance*.

The idea of cognitive dissonance must be expanded to include the dissonance between culture-in-the-mind and culture-on-the-ground.

A fateful meeting occurred on the morning of October 12, 1492. After a long and difficult voyage, Christopher Columbus and his crew arrived in the islands of the West Indies and lowered their anchor. Columbus donned his best scarlet doublet. His officers too dressed up. Each carried a sword. They got into their boats and rowed ashore. As they disembarked from their boats, they stood face to face with a small group of Taino Indians. Never, perhaps, had any people been as surprised as were the Taino. Neither side had any clue about what meanings might underlie the actions of the other.

Although such meetings had occurred many times before, the image of Columbus, decked out in red, landing on the shore of a tropical island and meeting naked Americans is surely the prototype for this situation.

Columbus brought an elaborate culture with him—both things and ideas. The Tainos' things were simpler, but their ideas were just as elaborate—and very different. The two sides had no way of communicating those meanings beyond basic animal gestures like friendliness and aggression. Most gestures are as cultural as language—and therefore unreadable by and alien to people of other cultural traditions.

The Taino and the Spaniards had intruded not merely into one another's space but into one another's ways of thought. The boundaries of both were forcefully expanded. Each tried to cram the new situation into the crannies of what they already knew— tried to explain the new situation with ideas that they had harbored before the event.

Whenever peoples of different cultural traditions come into contact, their two sets of ideas come into conflict. Whatever happens can now be interpreted in at least two ways. Tellingly, each way is largely unknown to the other party. The two ways may be contradictory even when they are known.

Columbus and the Taino found themselves in a situation of both cognitive and cultural dissonance. Not only were there two views of the situation playing themselves out, but the situation itself introduced dissonance into the minds of each.

The basis of *cognitive dissonance* is that people are uncomfortable if some of their knowledge and ideas are in conflict with other parts of their knowledge and ideas. Such contradiction imposes psychological conflict. People therefore search for consonance among the things that they know and do—they strive to reduce the dissonance in their lives.

The basic idea of *cultural dissonance* is that if the basic premises that underlie the thoughts of two interacting groups are not congruent, the lack of understanding between them is likely to intensify into a degree of misunderstanding that only flight, the use of force, or immense adaptations can overcome.

The experience of cultural dissonance is sharper if people's old ways work predictably to maintain subsistence and survival and to increase pleasure. The better the old ways mesh with the physical environment, the more painful they are to change. The necessarily limited perspective implied in the older ways makes the new ways seem wasteful or evil. To such people, adopting new ways means giving up activities that do not merely provide safety and pleasure, but seem to be part of the natural world. Efficiency is beside the point if security cannot be assured. Going against what people perceive as "nature" seems foolish and dangerous.

Cultural dissonance can occur between generations in times of very rapid social and cultural change like the 1960s in the United States, or when children grow up in a cultural environment that their parents do not share or understand and cannot use effectively—the dissonance between immigrants and their "native-born" children. Such dissonance can also be found between classes, between ethnic groups, and between nations. Perhaps the most poignant form of cultural dissonance is that which goes with colonialism. Differences between the culture of the colonizers and the cultures of the colonized can be difficult and painful for both.

FINDING COMMON GROUND

The usual mode of rapprochement between two uncomprehending cultures seems to be that people wall off a small area where the cultures most obviously overlap. Within that small compound, they develop, at least minimally, a "meeting culture." Insofar as that is successful, it leaves the rest of both cultures, behind their respective walls, as nearly intact as possible. Each now keeps many of its lifeways behind its wall, in an area that both peoples think is not known to the other side. (Even when it is known perfectly well, it may remain private.) Of course such efforts at maintenance can never be permanently successful—nevertheless, the attempts are made, and people tell themselves that, behind the wall, things are what they always were. For many decades even anthropologists were taken in by that particular piece of fiction. Both missionaries and colonial officials find such a wall threatening. Both, each in its way, keeps trying to breach the walls. The people behind the walls try to build them higher—in the process changing who they are and what they are doing.

New information that is in conflict with information we already have is notoriously difficult even to grasp, let alone assimilate and approve. Every teacher has to help students learn to question their premises in order that new things can be learned. Scientists or judges—and anthropologists—all have at least some trouble fitting in new ideas. New information is almost surely dissonant, in some degree. The dissonance is likely to increase people's insecurity, raise their caution, and perhaps excite their distrust. Some types of new information are easier to synchronize with the older information than others. But if there is an abyss of meaning between the premises underlying the traditional information and those underlying the new information, such synchronization is difficult.

In the presence of dissonance created by new information, there are several things that people can do. They can ignore the new information—deny that it is there. Denial is the simplest of the defense mechanisms, but it doesn't work very well because it estranges one from reality. It takes a lot of denial to say that something is not there if you can see it and smell it.

People may fight to do away with the new things, ideas, or people. Such a fight can take several forms. It turns up in the machinations of the French Academy as it tries to cleanse the French language of all Anglicisms. It turns up in uprisings that seek to drive out the intruders, such as the Tlingit uprisings against the Russian colonists in Alaska in the late 1700s and early 1800s. It turns up in irrational cult behavior in the service of some imagined new situation in which the dissonance magically disappears; this happened with the Ghost Dance. (This latter form is an example of what anthropologists have traditionally called nativistic movements.)

People can bring the old ideas and the new ideas into a single system, but it takes a great deal of creativity. By first learning what the differences are, then admitting that they exist, and then learning to adapt to the differences, everything may be made consonant. Once that creativity has triumphed—and once the amalgam has been accepted—it is impossible to go back to the older set of ideas. A true culture change has in fact occurred.

COLONIALISM

Colonialism is rife with both cultural and cognitive dissonance. The expanding Europeans, in the years after 1400, were following incremental action chains in which they readily accepted their innovations because they made perfect sense from the standpoint of their premises, their prior activities, and their ambitions. From the standpoint of the rest of the world, however, European expansion was a series of disasters.

First the Portuguese and Spanish began overseas expansion; the Dutch, French, and English soon followed. Just as important—and just as fateful for world history—was the overland expansion of the Russians, first against the Turkic peoples of central Asia, then on to the herding and hunting peoples who lived along the eastern shores of Siberia; they then took to the sea, expanding into Alaska, and on down the Pacific Coast until finally, just south of San Francisco, they had extended themselves so far that they had to turn back.

The problem of colonialism is complicated by the fact that the colonizers can bring only a small fraction of their material culture and their social culture with them. Thus, the people who have been hit from outside have limited opportunities to learn the culture of the newcomers. At the same time, the conquerors bring *all* of their ideas with them. Yet most of those ideas are not only invisible to the native peoples but unconscious to the conquerors themselves—it has never occurred to any of them that there are other ideas to hold. The native peoples can know only what they see of the behavior of those incomers. The complex cultural entity that underlies the behavior of the strangers is totally invisible to them. Their only option is to try to understand the behavior of the newcomers—as well as their own behavior in the new situation—in the light of what they can observe and what they already know.

Another type of cultural dissonance may become relevant: both dissonance and turbulence are *a priori* built into the cultures of the colonizers and other developed peoples to a degree never experienced by those who are being colonized. Every day more and more effective communication devices expose the people of the developed world to more and more ideas and customs—many of them foreign, many innovative. There is so much culture available to people in the developed world that no one person within it, and no single group of persons, can even know about all of it, let alone experience all of it or assimilate much of it.

The hallmark of a large-scale culture is that everybody in it must make choices. The choices are likely to make any one person's "lifestyle" (a word deplored by some anthropologists, but needed to comprehend complex cultures) more or less dissonant with the choices made by others. Each of us, as a result, has to struggle on the one hand to achieve our own consonance among the choices we have in fact made, and on the other to find modes of living in the same space as people who have opted for utterly different lifestyles.

Said another way, many people from complex cultures make certain choices, reject everything else in their cultural milieu, and continue with their lives—falling utterly out of touch with their neighbors who have made different choices. This has become so much today's mode of adjusting that we sometimes no longer have any "feel" for a holistic culture shared by all—one that hangs together and makes us hang together with the other people in our geographical community. It is sometimes asked, "Does the United States even *have* 'a culture'?"

Undoubtedly, as the effectiveness of communication devices grows, this kind of cultural dissonance will continue to grow. Cultural dissonance may thus be the only game in what some scholars call by the ugly term post-modern society. The situation can be summarized in Figure 11–1

In a colonial situation, dissonance is reinforced by political

FIGURE 11–1

Simple Societies, Colonial Societies, and Complex societies

	Simple Societies of the Past	Colonialism	Complex Emerging Societies
The Problem	How to survive and to enjoy	Two cultural points of view of survival and enjoyment; one is dominant over the other	Many components of culture, from which a person is expected to choose, then to make sense of the totality of his or her choices
Some Solutions	Everybody subscribes to the same ideas	Adjustment by both groups to ideas of the other, but the people of the subordinate group do most of the adjusting	A new kind of social structure in which cultures of many individuals are not consonant with one another; the dissonance becomes part of the system
Resulting Policy	A unitary culture	(1) living together while remaining different; (2) assimilation	Primacy of the person and a policy of support for human rights

power. Indeed, colonialism can be defined as a situation in which two or more cultures reach a more or less successful working misunderstanding. There are some areas—especially political and economic areas—in which the ideas of the colonial power are made dominant by force or the threat of it. The colonized people must adjust, with more or less pain. However, other areas—kinship, family, cooking, sometimes religion—are walled off. Each group can go its own way, caring little about the other group. The walled-off part of the native culture is more likely to be attacked by missionaries than by colonial governments; but it is a truism that colonial governments and missions often work together—for the simple reason that the two share many cultural ideas. (At least they can speak their native language to one another.)

Thus, culture contact is shaped by the clash of ideas that two or more different peoples hold when they are in direct contact. Each group of people actively avoids situations and information that lead to dissonance if they can do so. The most difficult part of the clash comes from the secret or unconscious parts—differences of the axioms or premises on which each of the two base their reasoning. These axioms are difficult to examine because they are either out of awareness until they are challenged or else they seem like propositions about the natural world. The incoming group (even an incoming anthropologist) finds them difficult, not only because they are alien but more powerfully because one has to make one's own hidden premises conscious before one can entertain new ones.

When the colonial kind of dissonance is found, Westerners have a tendency to call the lower-ranking people stupid for holding such ideas and "being unable to learn anything"; or they get out their guns; or they establish ways to "help" them or to "civilize" them; these usually take the form of charity, and usually make matters worse because psychological needs are not met.

From the standpoint of the people who are living with the dissonance, what has happened is that outsiders have ruined their way of life. They feel—and say—that if the outsiders and the changes they brought would just go away, things could be just great again. Yet almost without exception these people want *some* of the culture that the incomers brought with them. If the newcomers "just go away" those new valuable things go with them. A dilemma lurks there.

Dissonance in a culture is in some ways the opposite of recon-texting. It most often occurs when some imported idea or culture element creates a situation in which things no longer "make sense"—they do not fit together in the way they did before. The impact of the Western world on various non-Western societies in the years after 1400 are the anthropologists' favorite realm for studying dissonance.

We are now in a position to make a distinction among social process, history, and evolution. The part of social process that concerns us here—and it is much of it—is cyclical. When conditions change in either the physical or the cultural environment, the cycle changes. If the processes are not altered, they plunge over a cusp. That plunge is itself a change, and the cycle must adapt to it. A few cycles (such as the Tiv political cycle described earlier) may institutionalize the plunge over the cusp. But other processes are altered after the plunge, as people adapt their institutions to new sociocultural surroundings.

History, on the other hand, is a chronological statement of those events that triggered the changes—the specific form that events took as the cycles shifted from one process to a different one. A new cycle—more or less closely related to the old one—is formed.

CULTURAL EVOLUTION

Cultural evolution is the relationship of the old cycle to the new cycle. That is to say, when the change that created the new cycle is such that it is impossible—or at least not feasible—to return to the earlier state (a situation equivalent to gene loss), then evolution has occurred. Coevolution does not depend merely on genetic changes. It depends equally on loss of culture traits. It is such loss that clinches evolution, because it makes it so that you can't go home again.

This new situation is achieved genetically when new genes drive out old ones because they have greater survivor value. It is achieved culturally when one set of culture traits drives out another because the new traits make life simpler and are more rewarding. The two work together whenever culture-trait loss affects patterns of reproduction or whenever gene loss affects cultural choices.

This sequence is seen in Figure 11–2, which I have recast from an earlier model.[2] The repeating cycle is an oval of the sort that students in earlier times who had to deal with the old Palmer method of penmanship will instantly recognize as "ovals in place." The goal is to write one oval over another in precisely the same track, with no changes from one oval to the next. However, as anybody who has ever tried it knows, that is almost impossible. With each oval, the relationship between the cycle and the paper (control space) changes slightly. Either the ovals do not in fact overlap or the control space has to be crumpled and stretched to make them do so.

The differences from one oval to the next are likely to center at specific points. We can say that the points of crossing and recrossing in the diagram stand for "catastrophe." Thereupon, the new "oval in place" is readily formed. As one shifts body position, or the arm gets tired, or something jars the desk, or the paper moves and crumples, the ovals proceed across the page as evolution proceeds through time. Looked at in three dimensions, the oval has become an irregular spiral.

The necessary relationship among the event chains and cycles of social life, the events of history, and the spiral of evolution are in an analogous relationship.

There is an important lesson to be learned from all this: social changes that actually do occur should be studied in a context that

FIGURE 11–2
Cultural Cycles and Evolution

considers all those that *might* occur. We must look into the possibilities derived from our models (those provided here and more sophisticated ones), and not stop merely with what in fact has happened historically or ethnographically or psychologically. Science does not have to learn from experience. Scientists figure out how things work, and then get into the rhythms of those processes and let the processes achieve their aims for them. It is a matter of understanding the process (ovals in place) which is compounded of many variable processes, not just history (a single chain of catastrophes). The study of history is the study of only one type of process. Again to paraphrase Gertrude Stein: process is what happens all the time; history is what happens all the time from time to time. And evolution is what happens that makes it impossible to happen still another time.

Part III

Working with Culture

If culture were just a tool kit, we could redesign it at will as we can other tools. But the idea dimension of culture, lodged in many heads, sneaks stealthily past any redesigner. A cultural tradition is protean.

There is obviously a gap between social science and the "real world"— an error or omission in recontexting. In fact, there are two gaps: First, how do we recontext the ideas and understandings of real people into social science? Second, how do we recontext the findings of social science into the real world so that the undoubted advances in social science can be given sensible relevance?

Story and stories are a key to such recontexting. People examine cultural processes that they do not understand in terms of stories—just as they see mystical religious ideas in terms of myth. Once we succeed in recontexting cultural values into social science and the insights of social science into the real world, we stand a better chance of getting our simulations and our scenarios of the future more nearly right. If we actually get them right, our visions will have become more than some mere yearning for harmony or Utopia.

Chapter 12

Beyond Fieldwork

U ntil the end of the eighteenth century—indeed, until well into the nineteenth—any links between philosophy (as well as its heirs, the social sciences) and the concerns of everyday life were directed solely toward improving everyday life. Philosophers devised ways in which they thought the world could be made better. Few of them asked for facts about the squalors they wanted to correct. (Vico was probably an exception—there are undoubtedly others.) Although their efforts sometimes led to action, they seldom led to data gathering; thus their programs could not be based on situations in the real world.[1] The early reformers had nothing—no information about the nature of the system they were working with—between their goals and their action.

Then, in the very late nineteenth century, a few daring anthropologists discovered fieldwork, an idea based on the same premise as the old Cadillac ads that said, "Ask the man who owns one!" In the decades that followed, almost all cultural anthropologists, and some political scientists and a few sociologists, took that road. (To this day, far too many social scientists—even some anthropologists—draw impeccable samples of respondents, and then ask unconsidered questions of the people who fall into their

147

samples, a process that can yield only statistifiable answers to silly questions.)

Fieldwork was a first attempt to recontext ideas as they are actually held in the real world—especially in foreign cultural traditions—into the emerging world of social science. It is the best way so far discovered, in spite of the fact that it remains an art with many built-in traps.

SOCIAL SCIENCE AFTER FIELDWORK

Fieldwork, however, is not the last word. We have to take the next step: to find some means to assure that we know not only the "facts" that we observe but also the *arrangement* and *interpretation* given to those facts by the people themselves. One of the best ways to check on that is to learn the language of those people—if you can talk to them about the intricacies of your discoveries, and they understand what you are talking about, it's a sign you have it right. Even that, however, is not full insurance against importing your own ways of arranging data into your analysis. We need at least one more step.

That next step, it seems to me, will be twofold. We must, first of all, get the ways that the people themselves see the structures and processes of their own culture into our data—I believe no anthropologist would disagree with that. But that is the easy part. The more difficult part is to get the reading audience of the author's own culture to understand the data *and the processes* of the subject peoples. This is difficult for both the writer and the readers.

How, to put it differently, do we engage people, at a gut level, in the findings of social science? And, even prior to that, how can we be sure that social scientists will find better ways—less distorting ways—to engage *themselves*, as social scientists, in the "findings" of the people they study?

The communication gap between social science and the "real world" is wider than we think. Yet how, without good communication, can the worthwhile and valuable findings of social science—those that will make adapting to the real world easier and more rewarding—be utilized? And how can the findings of real people out there (who have some good ideas and some ways of doing and behaving that deserve to be emulated) be discovered and then utilized in social science?

I am *not* asking social scientists to give up their categories of thought—their definitions of social class and ethnicity and gender and all the other categories they use to spin into insight whatever "facts" they can statisticize—such studies tell us a lot. I am, however, asking them to ponder the effectiveness of their communication—first with the people who are the sources of their data as they communicate among themselves, and then with the consumers (as it were) of their findings.

THE FIELD OF STORY STUDIES

As this is being written, the U.S. Congress is debating the issues of health care. Anecdotes about the defects of the present system occupy center stage. When people give evidence to committees and fact-finding commissions, they tell their stories. It is in those stories that the power lies; the stories contain data, but they also contain the popular analyses of the process that leads to frustrations or victories. In those stories, Congress can observe the struggle of the many forces and issues that they must contend with. The stories—if we learn to listen to the values that they embody and the cultural processes that they assume (indeed axiomize)—can deepen our understanding to the point where we are no longer dependent on luck, as Robert Owen or Lenin were, to get from the vision to the performance.

Today's anthropologists, listening to literary critics, have begun to use the power of story as an assistant in making that leap. Although anthropologists (at least since Fraser and Boas) have insisted on the importance of folk tales and songs, story is nevertheless a blind spot in our study of our own cultural tradition—even though we devour so many stories in the form of books, plays, television shows, and political argument. Jokes are stories. So are biographies. So are allegories, fables, sagas, legends, myths, histories, parables—even slogans. Anthropology needs professional, developed ways to encompass the subtleties of story.

Anthropology has long carried on a flirtation with literature and literary criticism. I remember the flirtation between British

anthropology and the "new criticism" at Cambridge University—
F. R. Leavis and all that—which was of great moment in British
anthropology in the early 1950s, although as far as I know it did
not produce any published residue. I associate that movement
with Godfrey Lienhardt, who was a student and friend of F. R.
Leavis. Its major thrust was the conviction that a batch of fieldwork information is like a literary text in that it should be examined for itself, not for the personalities who wrote it or even the
environmental forces that helped to shape it. It existed in its own
right.

Today, a new interest in literary criticism brings the insights of
specialized students of literature into play in communicating
between social science and real people. The process is *in medias res*
and has not really happened yet. To go into this topic as fully as I
hope to do later would draw me too far from the focal point of
this book. However, one of this book's foci is on the values and
structure of story, including the cultural processes revealed by
story.

Does such a concern with story take us the next step beyond
fieldwork? Certainly it may help.

People live by stories—they use stories to organize and store
cultural traditions. Changes in people's stories not only reflect
changes in cultural reality; they can actually create them. That is
why politicians are traditionally said to distrust poets. A story or
poem or song allows ordinary people—the traditional "Every-
man"—to see things anew, even to detect and avoid cultural traps.
With stories and poems, people can work cultural changes in
areas that they cannot even think about *except* as stories.

Social scientists, especially anthropologists, ignore stories at
their peril. Yet the scholarship about story is strangely flabby.
Story is so basic in our minds—and so categorized—that we do
not even put an entry on story in our encyclopedias: if you look
up "story" in the *1987 World Book*, you find nothing. There is no
"story" entry in the 1962 *Encyclopaedia Britannica*; nor in the *Encyclopedia of the Social Sciences*. The 1992 *Grolier Electronic Encyclopedia* has an entry for "short story" but none for story. Moreover, if
you look in your local library, you are likely to find that its hold-
ings under "story" focus around the librarian's art of telling stories to children—an important educational topic, but not one that

is much help if you are seeking to understand the basic structure and cultural purpose of story.

Story is not exactly neglected in the Western cultural tradition, but it has been relegated to a corner of our minds, called *fiction*, and confused with lies. But story is like play. Nobody has ever succeeded in categorizing play as a type of something else—play is a basic "unit" entity of animal behavior. Just so, story is a basic unit in cultural behavior.

Only recently have scholars begun to get interested in comparing our stories, and our ideas of story, with the stories of other peoples and their ideas about and uses of stories. Sir James Fraser sort of did it in *The Golden Bough*, and such scholars as Mircea Eliade have done it. But the mainstream of cultural anthropology is only just beginning to ask: How do *we* use stories? How do other peoples use stories?

First, we had better take our own view of story: in Western cultures, story has gotten mixed up with fiction, although we all know that some stories are true (whatever "truth" may be made to mean). At another level, of course, we also know that fiction is a way to delve deeper into truth than any mere account of what actually happened can do. Myth—origin story—can explain whole reaches of cultural tradition that are not susceptible to any other kind of explanation.

History is a story on which we have come to put very specific kinds of limitation. For no matter how gripping the story in history, no matter how vital the lessons that might be learned, history's story should correspond with the "facts" as we have defined *facts*. Fiction is not hampered by such a need for "facts." Myths demand verisimilitude, but they certainly are not to be judged by the same standards of truth used for history. A glance at the tradition of official Chinese "histories" shows some of the problems: all the "facts" have been corrected to "supposed-tos." Replacing what actually happened with what should have happened is common for a lot of us. The psychoanalysts call this "working through."

It has even been said that ethnographers write "stories" about the people they study. True enough—but the people who say that tend to confuse story with fiction, and thereby to denounce what they consider to be inadequate ethnography. The implication is that the ethnographer made up his stories out of whole cloth.

Obviously, ethnographers don't. They may have confused their own unconscious patterns with the patterns behind somebody else's story, but they *didn't* make the story up. The real question, thus, is whether the ethnographer made up the *arrangement* of the facts.

This issue takes on even greater interest when the ethnographer creates theory (a specialized form of story).

People, in every cultural tradition ever explored, tell stories. Libraries are full of collections of folktales from all over the world (although references to them are not likely to be catalogued under "story"). Anthropologists (and other people) find folktales easy to collect. People are usually not reticent about telling them; ethnographers can study the language in the process of collecting them; they can even find publishers for them. Yet few of those collections explore the deeper meanings to be found within or behind the tales—and none is likely to inquire about the structure of the tales. When they are retold for children, they are likely to be muffled with the morality (often alien to the original story) that the grown-up storyteller thinks that children in his own culture should soak up.

We have (in Chapter 7) already talked about Vladimir Propp, who in the early part of the twentieth century[2] set the study of story into a new key. The point here is to make sure that we grasp the importance of stories in allowing people to grasp their own culture, to think about it creatively and constructively, and to communicate it—both its values and its processes—to an ethnographer.

Propp found that all the stories in his collection of Russian fairy tales followed the same pattern. His contribution allows us to understand that stories are the mechanism by which the action chains of social and cultural process are examined and discussed by the people who live out those action chains. Stories proceed from one event to the next, following a master formula for action chains: growth, travel, discovery—all are there and all come in the same order. Not only does one event both set and limit the possibilities for the next, but the meaning of an event depends on its place in the course of events. The course of a story may follow the biological growth and aging of the characters, the limitations built into the characters by the processes of matter and of life, the guidance and traps suffered by the characters as a result of the workings of their cultural traditions, the choices that the characters make, and the reactions of other characters in the story to those choices.

Thus, every story follows an action chain—and the number of action chains that stories may follow is not only finite, it is small. The action chain of a story resembles the action chains of "real life." Indeed, a story provides a stunning example of recontexting: elements of real life are separated out, perhaps simplified, and then recontexted into a made-up story that informs a tale, a play, a myth, a novel. In the recontexted form, people can bear to look at—even enjoy looking at—situations that they could not muster the courage to face in the larger theater of their own lives, where decisions once taken have to be carried out, not just imagined. Stories are thus primitive but effective forms of simulation.

Stories are gripping not merely because we can identify with the characters, but perhaps even more because we understand the difficulties of the characters' choices, empathize with their need to make them, and learn more about the pattern.

Feeling that you *have* to know "what happens next" means finding out which choice the character makes, what particular path the action chain will follow. The agony or ease of carrying forward that choice, seeing the results of choice and the options that choosing opens or closes—these are the rewards of story. Sometimes stories are disturbing. The way the particulars of the story take us through some aspects of the human condition provide its power. But the uniqueness of this particular story—this version of the pattern—rewards us by teaching us new avatars of the pattern.

The story, in other words, recontexts the choices of life. It allows people to examine, at a safe distance, the results of their choices before anything has actually taken place. The fate of each character is rolled up in the choices he or she makes, in the reactions of other characters, and in the cultural options that are released or shut down by the action. The action chain of the story instructs us about the action chains we face daily in the more inclusive—and more definitive and demanding, more "real"—context of our lives.

Propp worked on a set of Russian fairy tales.[3] The structure of the tales in his series involves a series of thirty-nine possible

FIGURE 12–1

Action Chain of Propp's Fairy Tales

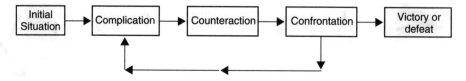

actions or events. Instead of recapping them here, I shall simplify them into the kind of action chain we examined in Part II of this book.

A storyteller has to inform the audience of what the initial situation is, to "set it up." In "real life," of course, every situation is a stage of an ongoing process—something leads up to every situation. The storyteller has to make an important decision here: do I tell about what happened before (called *backstory* by the people who teach college students to write fiction)? Do I decide that what went before is irrelevant and never mention it? Or am I skillful enough to structure the events of my story in such a way that what led up to the story is never missed? Backstory, unless it is handled very deftly, slows down the flow of the "now" story—may even bring it to an abrupt halt from which it may never again move forward. A few skillful storytellers can get away with flashbacks, but this takes great mastery. Thus, setting the initial situation is one of the trickiest parts of learning to tell or write stories.

Yet many people who work with stories "know" the back-story. I am reminded of the way diviners work among the Tiv. Tiv usually try to consult diviners at some distance from their homes, who cannot possibly know the details of the questioner's problem. What they do not realize is that when they go to diviners, they carry their backstories with them. If an older man and a younger man approach a diviner, the diviner turns to the younger man and asks, "What's wrong with your wife?" If five or so men all the same age approach the same diviner, he asks, "What happened to your age-mate?"

Diviners, first having established their *bona fides* by asking the right question about backstory, then have subtle but effective ways of getting details about what led to the distress about which they are now consulting. Moreover, they know the pattern, and hence how the story is likely to proceed. The diviner, knowing pretty well how the story goes, can give advice about what one can do to make the story proceed according to the pattern.[4]

My point is a simple one: the fieldworker must first of all learn enough to be able to detect backstory in the way the diviners do. He must know the process, then fit the events into it.

Propp offers seven items that may be involved in setting up the initial situation (the backstory and/or first incident) of one of those tales:

1. one of the family members absents himself
2. an interdiction is addressed to the hero
3. the interdiction is violated
4. the villain tries a reconnaissance in search of important information
5. the villain gets such information about his victim
6. the villain attempts to deceive the victim so that he can get possession either of the person or the belongings of the victim
7. the victim submits to the deception of his enemy.

Note that events 2 and 3 may be linked or amalgamated in a single incident, as is also the case with 4 and 5, or 6 and 7.

The best storytellers set forth as many of these elements as they will need simply and quickly—the best can do it in a sentence or two. Only when this kind of backdrop is in place can the story's events begin to unfold.

Next, in the complication phase, either the villain causes harm to some member of the hero's family, or a member of the family becomes aware that he or she lacks something desirable. When that misfortune or lack is made known to the hero, the hero is either sent out to do something about it or decides independently to go do something about it. Heroes, we discover, can be either victims or seekers. If the hero is a seeker, he either agrees to or instigates some sort of counteraction against the villain. He leaves home, and is tested or attacked as many times as the storyteller likes. (At this point a cycling or repetitive segment may be added to the story line, which is otherwise a trajectory.) In many of the fairy tales, the hero comes into possession of a magic agent. The hero is thereupon led (often by the magic agent) to the object he is seeking.

At this point in the process, there is a confrontation: the hero and the villain fight. The hero may be branded, but the villain is defeated. With the victory or defeat, the original lack that was set forth is corrected.

This simplification of Propp's outlines makes it clear how the story "should" go.

The beauty of this form is that every story in which the action chain is used can be different from every other story—just as each cultural tradition can be both different from and the same as others or each personality different from but the same as others. Every storyteller can embellish it for a particular audience. But the process remains steadfastly in place. Creativity and originality are found in the specifics, not in the process. New process may be possible in the folktale mode, but only in times of cultural turmoil when new challenges face a people so that the old way of solving problems no longer works.

A human life, or series of lives, is thus not only a story but is the raw material for all stories. A good story—even a joke—illuminates life. The story *is* life, usually reduced in its dimensions. Any particular life is a whole bunch of stories intertwined so that each story affects all the others.

Old people, in processes usually summed as reminiscence, put their life histories into story form. Using the patterns established by the view of the life course that holds in their cultural tradition, they first perceive, and then examine, the processes of their own lives, and the point that they have reached. Indeed, they adjust and adapt their memories into stories that they can justify, that they consider interesting—a life worth having led. When people cannot do that, their lives seem futile to them and despair sets in.

Stories—and story processes—can also delineate cultural traps. Escapes from the machinations of a villain may be replaced with overcoming cultural traps. Stories and games built around them show in simplified form, outside ourselves, what culture traps await us and what they do to us.

Science fiction provides a simple but instructive case. Indeed, a well-known science-fiction writer once told me that his craft involved knowledge of two disciplines, physics and anthropology, "and you can finesse the physics." The preparatory phase of a science-fiction story outlines either a fateful problem in the way the world works (it may be presented as a threat to the survival of the cosmos), or a society in which some cultural element that we formerly thought necessary, no matter how distasteful, is absent, or one in which some horrendous new piece of culture has been added that makes familiar patterns not only untenable, but destructive—that is to say, a cultural trap is revealed. The story then proceeds along a pattern—call it a formula—and ends up consoling us at the same time that it broadens our horizons.

My point here is that this kind of knowledge, derived from the analysis of the texts of stories, must be made an integral part of successful fieldwork—a sort of para-fieldwork.

However, we must remember that stories have at least two elements that may be lacking in real life: the audience and the storyteller.[5] It is their presence, and their interaction, that makes stories so dangerous to any existing social order.

The audience is important because all performances—at least, those that pre-date the mass media, which have complicated and may attenuate the lines of feedback—are social relationships between performer and audience. The reaction of the audience is the stimulus that drives the performer. The qualities of the performance are the stimuli that grasp and hold the audience. The very best story is futile if it is told to the wrong audience or in a style that may be suitable for some audience or other, but not for the audience at hand.

A successful storyteller adapts his complications, his counteractions, his confrontations not just to his audience but also to the subject he is dealing with. Because every story needs a teller, every storyteller has a problem with "voice." Who is the storyteller? How does it come about that he or she knows the story? Does the storyteller's identity warp the story? Without a teller there is no story—just as without an audience there is no story. And just as without an ethnographer there is no ethnography—except as audience the alien culture cannot be made to exist, not even to itself.

So the story is recontexted from the real world into the world of contemplation and enjoyment of propositions about the human condition.

In the interests of being "scientific," social scientists all too often fail to recognize the importance of story. They may leave out the characters; this makes it difficult for listeners to internalize the story, because that internalization is usually done by identification with or hatred of some character, and empathy for the way he or she solves problems that one has one's self faced. Margaret Mead once said that people will believe anything an anthropologist tells them as long as they are not asked to apply the lessons to themselves. That sets the problem: how can we help people empathize with social science discoveries at the same time that we disallow their using the social science to distance themselves from some of the uncomfortable truths that social science may reveal? How, in other words, can social science be successfully recontexted, especially when people, for their own comfort, do not want to hear discouraging or counterintuitive messages?

The task of fitting one's self into a story is the task of the listener or reader or viewer. However, the storyteller must cast the story in such a way that the listener will not desert him *because* he has successfully cast himself into the story.

We are thus left with creating the story of social science (both the theory and its popularization) so that the findings of social science can become an integral part of the everyday life of the culture that imbeds the social science. If I knew how to do that, I would be rich and famous.

Chapter 13

Simulation

When people strip away the entertainment value and symbolic nature of story in order to postulate possible outcomes of real-life choices, a different kind of recontexting occurs—simulation. Simulation, if it is done right, allows people to see from a safe distance some of the possible results of recontexting. It helps people observe and analyze situations. It is a handmaiden of any successful policy science. But how do you do it right?

Simulation can be used at a trivial level: some hairdressers offer a computerized try-the-new-hairdo-before-you-get-your-haircut service: your photo is fed into a computer which can thereupon show you, on screen, any number of hairdos applied to your particular face. You can then judge which cuts and which colors work best, and have the hairdresser make it real. The ads say that by using this method all disasters can be avoided.

Simulation is also used for instruction. Flight simulators have long been standard parts of training a pilot; war games and table-top strategy sessions have long been used by the armed forces. Technological processes can be checked out by simulation before they are put into practice. Many firms can save themselves millions of dollars by successful simulation. Astronauts learn to handle weightlessness as they simulate under water the activities they will carry out in space.

PROBLEMS OF CULTURAL SIMULATION

Simulation of *social* processes has had a spotty history. At least three reasons are evident.

1.   Some of us confuse even *trying* to carry out social simulation with questioning our political and religious institutions and hence with treachery, betrayal, and godlessness. Although social scientists are allowed to carp about the inadequacies of our social system, the moment we compare it with other systems without first condemning those other systems, we are suspect. It is hard to get rid of the idea that questioning or investigating our own system is tantamount to championing some other system.

2.   We muddy our simulations with our wishes and desires and values. Either consciously or unconsciously we bend the conditions so that the results of the simulation come out the way we, for whatever reason, want them to come out.

3.   Even when we consciously know better, we fail to separate the cultural environment from the natural environment. We unthinkingly assume that our cultural qualities are natural and eternal. Thus, without ever investigating them, we align the social processes we are simulating with the premises underlying our logic rather than making them the subject of the questions we are investigating and testing. That is what simulation ought to do— check out the validity of our premises.

SIMULATION AND POLICY SCIENCE

Using what we know about social and cultural processes as the basis for policy decisions has never been taken seriously by anyone except a few social scientists. Skilled diplomats do, of course, look ahead to possible foreign reactions to certain decisions, but they usually muddy that activity by sticking to a closed-ended question: "What's in the interests of the United States?" for example, instead of an open-ended one: "What has created this problem and what has to be adjusted before it can be solved?" Many skilled managers understand the motives of their work force even as they choose to follow the short-term dictates of economic advantage instead of the longer-term advantages of a more satisfying cultural context for their employees.

Examining processes is hard to do specifically because it demands that we rise above all sides of any argument in order to look at the argument itself. We have been taught to consider our side in terms of moral values. But when we look at both sides, the moral dimension takes a back seat; it is replaced with an operational dimension—maybe we can do something to reduce the conflict instead of merely trying to win it. The disappearance of familiar morality is disconcerting. But if we cannot question ideas that are presented in unwaveringly moral terms—that is, if we are taught that it is wrongheaded or sinful to question them—then we cannot get to the more inclusive level. Hence we cannot understand the total problem.

The result is that most social scientists have few models for simulating social action. Economists have been more successful than the rest of us because they have been better able to escape the moral dimension and to find something that can unequivocally be counted. Some of their economic indicators would seem to be useful, for all that many economists themselves insist that none is to be taken without qualification.

Past attempts to find *social* indicators have, however, not been successful. Part of the reason may have to do with discovering (or, better, making up) quantifiable categories of culture or social action in the sense that economists have been able to apply quantifiable categories to their data on the movement of money. But an even greater part comes from being unable to escape from one side within the problem to look at the problem as a whole. That inability is constantly refueled by fear of political expulsion.

Our job is to dare to break away from the "side" that our people tell us we should remain loyal to. Only if we can break such low-level loyalties and speak for the species can we apply the benefits of simulation to wider ranges of social and cultural life.

How, in other words, do we get rid of the association between social process and ideology? How can we examine the process as a whole instead of half the process seen through a veil of ideology? Is the answer to find a more fruitful ideology that derives from the process itself? How do we devise ways of detecting hidden ideologies that warp our simulations and make them come out as we want them to? With what do we replace the notion that social processes are somehow natural, like bodily growth and aging? How do we reassure ourselves that some social processes *can* be adjusted without our taking over the tasks of God or giving people crazy and impossible ideas? And, perhaps most difficult of all, how do we detect the opportunities for stepping up from side-taking—when the other side may be waiting for us to make a move of that sort so that they can destroy us and "win" the situation in their own narrow terms, instead of coming to terms with it and finding a solution that would profit the entire species?

It may be that this is a triadic problem. That is to say, maybe we need a third party in order to solve the problem, in precisely the same way that a judge is a third party solving problems of dyadic conflict. However, if the third party lacks the power to enforce decisions, only those problems will be solved that both sides want solved.

Process analysis should be at the heart of simulation of social policy. Do we have to spend almost a century and untold human misery fooling around with ideas like communism to find out not only *that* they don't work, but *why* they don't work? Or, come to that, do we have to limit our vision in such a way that the only imaginable alternative to communism is market capitalism?[1]

Policy science is an activity that, at the present time, has as many definitions as it has practitioners. Too often it examines problems out of their cultural context; when answers arrived at in such play space are fed back into the real world, all sorts of realities intrude to throw out the answers into doubt. All those practitioners share the conviction that they cannot try to predict precisely what is going to happen—that's fortune telling. Rather, their task is to anticipate everything that *might* happen—indeed, that *can* happen, given specific social and technical conditions. Only when we anticipate all possibilities can contingency plans—a good Plan B to fall back on when Plan A falls through—be made confidently.

Anthropologists have at least two contributions to make to policy science if they can change their focus sufficiently to make them. They can undertake a thorough study of the *outcomes* of actual past decisions, as set forth in the historical and ethnographic records. Specifically, they can ask, what happens when patterns of trajectory and cycle are interfered with? History does not repeat itself—but patterns do. By studying history comparatively, as many examples of cultural process, we can detect the workings of the cultural system rather than attributing the outcomes to the machinations of persons or the muscle-flexing of political movements. We could establish categories of errors, then help to simulate many possibilities that avoid those errors. And anthropologists can help to formulate rules for determining just how cultural processes are similar to, and how they are different from, natural processes like aging. Action chains, after all, can help us decide whether a particular practitioner would be wiser to focus on some given action rather than on some other action.

The basic question in seeking policy is "What might happen *if. . .* ?" Thus, policy science is about action chains—how doing one thing leads to doing another. Action chains become parts of cultural patterns. As patterns work—and as they work unforeseen changes as well as intended changes—they become the norm. Traps and possible turmoil may be made evident. Our goal is to find out as much as we can ahead of time about what cultural traps are lurking where, and which are likely to get us hopelessly locked in. Preliminary analysis of possible action chains—based on models derived from history and ethnography—will help in that effort.

THE ROLE OF ANTHROPOLOGY

Anthropology can help the policy sciences include consideration of the unconscious factors that accompany the participation of individual persons in action chains. Somebody had to find a vaccine for polio—but why Jonas Salk, proceeding as he did? What processes direct scientific creativity? Just so, somebody had to emerge in Germany in the late 1920s to counter the anomie that then permeated German life, but why Hitler? Is nationalistic dictatorship a virus, or are we merely in the same kind of trap that the ancient Greeks encountered when they failed to find cultural devices that would allow their city-states to coexist without trying to destroy one another?

Anthropologists can help discover the proper axioms of a policy science. First of all, policy science should assume humans beings that work by feedback; it should assume dyads as the unit of society; it should assume that social triads can have an immense effect on dyads; it should set out to explore the possible outcomes of action chains, event chains, cycles, and cusp catastrophes until it can find better models.

One of the goals of anthropology—and hopefully of policy science as well—is to detect social traps so that we can get out of them or avoid getting into them. Today most of that is done by hunch and "feel." Hunch and empathy help, but they should not be the only strings to our bow. What do we add? First of all, a sophisticated kind of fieldwork. Only then can we begin to apply to social analysis the quantitative methodologies usually associated with statistics.

Statistical models can tell us a lot but they cannot, in themselves, detect when the data are out of sync with the reality they purport to analyze. Neither are they a very good way to release creativity and new thought, because nobody is actively sassing the statistician. Ethnographic models work, in part because real live people are talking back to the ethnographer. However once we learn by detailed inquiry precisely what the problems are, statistical models become essential. Statistics needs to be informed by the right questions. Those right questions *may* be the result of hunches. However, fieldwork and analysis of the complex correlations that can indeed be exposed by the statistics are essential.

COMPARISON

Anthropologists use comparatively few statistics, in large part because there are no banks of data for them to draw on—each of us must gather our own data. Instead we have, for many generations now, used an exercise called "comparison." Comparison is a useful exercise because it allows social scientists (and policy makers) to examine the way several different peoples, each with different cultural traditions, have handled situations similar to the one at hand. If we look at, say, many examples of people reducing risk in hunting and gathering, we find that food-sharing is a common form in many places. We can thereupon postulate that hunters and gatherers are likely to share food. We can then examine in detail what conditions are either present or absent when food-sharing is *not* to be found in that kind of society. So far, this kind of exercise has been carried out only on small problems in the complex societies. When will anthropologists learn to broaden their horizons and focus their communications so that policy makers can learn that it is worth their while to listen to what they have to say?

In short, I am calling for an amalgamation of some of the social sciences: anthropologists should be more like other social scientists, and those others should also be more like anthropologists. Although it is true that more anthropologists (including me) should get more statistically sophisticated, it is also true that other social scientists should pick up the anthropological quality of determining what the genuine question is instead of merely statistifying whatever data they happen to have. The computer age is making data available to everybody—but if the social scientists don't get on with the job of determining whether the available data fit the real problems, the data don't much matter. This is not a problem of data, but rather of creative thought.

We can, of course, use the traditional anthropological tool of comparison as a mode for examining immensely important questions that haunt us today: how many times in history (and whose history?) has submerged ethnicity emerged when empires fall? What are the implications? Do we really *need* another empire, or another kind of empire, to repress the horrors of ethnic conflicts? Can the repression of ethnicity occur without a centralized political power?

The comparative method has not been significantly used outside anthropology. But using it could help create a database from which a more sophisticated social science could emerge. And in precisely the same way, if anthropologists could find some way beyond comparison and statistics to *use* those databases, all of social science would be better off. With historical and ethnographic examples before us, some of the possible traps in any given situation can be more readily foreseen and perhaps forestalled.

The advantages of comparison are straightforward, but two

considerations have to be examined. First of all, most anthropological comparisons have in the past been made on the basis of morphologically described structures rather than processes. I am convinced that comparison of such structural snapshots is not very fruitful. We need, instead, the continuity of the processes revealed by moving pictures. Second, comparisons should no longer be considered a goal in themselves—as the end product. Anthropologists have to take an active role in the next step: the role of comparison in policy science. Indeed, they have to make themselves cogent to that weird congeries of social scientists who consider themselves policy people. If they can do that they will be heard. If they can't, they have nothing worthwhile to say.

If we are interested in, say, the destruction of the environment, first of all we should not assume that our problem is unique. The environment has been destroyed many times in the history and prehistory of humankind. The agricultural revolution came about because the hunting activities (as well, perhaps, as other events) had already brought about the destruction of the environment in which hunting societies were even possible. The industrial revolution occurred when the environment was so completely ruined that it led to the collapse of small-scale peasant farming. The destruction of the environment by early industrial society led to new modes of dealing with the environment. Indeed, had the terrestrial environment not been repeatedly destroyed, humankind might never have taken the risks involved first in leaving the secure mode of livelihood that hunting large mammals provided, and then later leaving the more treacherous but still predictable life of the small-scale family farm set into a small-scale community of intimately known neighbors.

We can then take all the examples we can find of destruction of the environment, overlap them (as cryptanalysts used to overlap the regularities found in encoded messages before computers completely took over the job), and come up with patterns. Within the patterns, we will almost surely find cycles. If we have several examples, we may be able to get a more extensive hold on how the pattern applies in any specific instance. We may make some headway in considering how we can solve this problem and proceed to the next.

SOME BASICS

Here, then, going back to the first chapter of this book, is a summary of some of the most basic preliminary requirements for the new anthropology that is emerging now that anthropology has been deprived its original niche, tucked somewhere in between anticolonialism and liberalism.

1.   Analysts have to begin with the nature of the human creature, admitting that the creature cannot for very long act against its own biological interests. They have to admit that those biological factors exist—which is hard for some people, who are led by some ideologies to postulate that such biological factors limit human spirituality, and hence failure to overcome them is moral failure. The model of the person who stores information outside himself in the form of culture—and the overpowering (because unthinking) way in which the person draws on that externally stored information—is the necessary beginning of such a view.

2.   Persons, in their deeds, follow "action chains" that are both goal-dominated and traditional. In many cases, the action chain involves deeds by two or more persons. An institution, or a group such as a corporation, can act as a "person" in the progressions of action chains.

3.   The dyad of such persons is the unit of society. That is to say, a part of each person's comparator is put into the external culture. No person can ever fully control a situation when he or she has to include the workings of other persons in order to complete the chain.

4.   Thereupon a "cultural tradition" springs up, based on the principles and ideas with which both try, more or less, to conform. The cultural tradition makes life more nearly predictable. Some persons will, of course, use the tradition to protect their personal winning strategies. However, every cultural tradition is finitely elastic: persons can stretch their own "advantage" only a certain distance before they are forced into social isolation. In this way, the cooperation implied in sociality takes hold. Which will the person decide to give up—the sociality or the advantage?

5.   There is a trap in such a cultural tradition—it may make you turn questions into dogma so that you don't have to answer them.

6.   A cultural tradition is manifest in the rules of every two-party event chain—and the parties may be nations or pacts of nations as well as persons. The purpose of the rules is to create profitable predictability. Those rules can change very fast. But there is an irony: one of the by-products of such rules is that they can be used to bolster an individual's entrenched position in the structure, which is the underside of cooperation.

7.   It was one of the earliest victories of social science that the interconnectedness of many different social institutions and forces came to be understood: if you change one thing, something else in the cultural tradition (perhaps everything) may also change. Therefore, the various social processes that go to make up the cultural tradition—processes that are recognized, and more or less willingly followed by the persons—affect one another even when they are not in conflict.

8.   Finally, we must always remember that all culture, including culturized social organization, is a tool kit just as surely as a screwdriver, a needle, an axe, or an atomic reactor are tools. We have not yet learned to treat social organization overtly like a tool. Our fears and our dogmas too often limit the uses to which we can put our social tools.

The goal of a new anthropology has to be first to understand how culture works, at all levels. If proscription is called for, then the next step must be to try to create judgments about cultural traditions and to help make decisions that will not be overwhelmed by the damaging reflexes of persons and cultural traditions.[2]

Another problem soon emerges in this new anthropology: it is difficult—maybe even impossible—to create culture that is tailor-made for specific situations. There are several reasons for this difficulty.

1.   It is difficult to control unconscious premises while we examine all possibilities. The major problem here is getting those unconscious premises up into our awareness—once they are out in the open, they *can* be held in suspension while the situation is examined in a new light. But exposing them takes a kind of creativity—and courage—that is rare; it is almost impossible to teach

because resistance to it is fueled by unconscious fears and we resist our own bravest efforts to get them out of the darkness.

2.   We may not see all the interconnections of a cultural tradition until after we have already embarked on one course of action or another.

3.   We have to overcome our wrongheaded need to control the processes we come to recognize rather than trusting them. Can we separate trusting the process from trusting the other side? Purposefully creating new cultural tradition is a quite different kind of exercise from remodeling what is already there. Not even heroic measures or dictators can control that kind of creativity. Yet it is something that, from time immemorial, has allowed human beings to adjust to changing situations. Ironically enough, it is also what heads them toward lock-ins.

4.   The processes of transformation are likely to be influenced unexpectedly—from left field, to use the baseball metaphor. In order to control cultural change totally, you have to control communication and recontexting. You can't do *that* without total thought control—and even dictatorship as we have known it is not an effective form of thought control. Indeed, dictatorship would seem to lead to active resistance to thought control. Dictators can make the price of action so high that people do not act, but they cannot keep people from sensing injustice or devising schemes to counteract it. Dictators can more nearly, but not entirely, devise schemes that make it prohibitively expensive in time, money, and life for people to put their ameliorative ideas into effect. But occasionally they run into people who identify with the species instead of just some fraction of it, whose altruism is such that they will put their lives on the line. The Sakharovs of this world—and there are many—will continue to take up stances supporting the rights of human beings. And those stances will continue to undermine thought control.

The irony, thus, is that we all need culture and depend on it—we are all involved in some cultural tradition—but we cannot control it totally. The moment we try too hard to control it, culture turns on us and destroys us.

People have, by surviving through the course of evolution, created something that is more powerful than themselves. Cultural tradition, although it works very differently and is far more subtle, is as strong as genetic inheritance. But because cultural tradition is capable of rapid change—Proteus is the god of culture—it sometimes seems evanescent. We can only try to understand how culture works and figure out how to live with it. Control will not work. To try to control culture is to prove once for all that you don't understand it and you are buckling under to it. To attempt to control culture is to admit weakness. What we *can* do is enrich it every time it turns on us.

And we can also begin to find out how culture works. In the past, we have used religious dogma—a small part of the cultural tradition even if, in some eras, it has been the leading one—to control ourselves so that we don't have to try to control culture. Now we need autonomy *and* understanding, a larger whole that so far moves faster than its analysts. That is what makes the achievement of autonomy difficult. We have to learn to become autonomous within the limitations imposed by culture, most often by a cultural tradition.

The only way to get around this intransigence of culture is by what can be termed "trained intuition." That means that we get used to looking for premises, we grow more comfortable with the counterintuitive without ever ceasing to question it, we begin to cast our social problems into the same terms as we cast technological problems, with full awareness of the subtle differences between the way physical principles work and the way culture works. While the first draft of this chapter was being written a hundred cars piled up on Highway I-15 north of San Bernardino, California. Broadcast savants and editorial writers said that we will soon have a technological answer for preventing this kind of disasters: radar or something of the sort. However when, during the same period, local and national commentators came to investigate ingrained cultural ways of doing things like medical treatment, they looked at it in terms of bad guys instead of as a dimension of a system that could be reformed if we were willing first to examine it and then to change some of our habits. Vested interests, selfishness, fear—they keep us even from trying to simulate some matters. Where are the simulations about a remodeled plan of health services for all people? If they are there, they have not escaped from the political wrangling and the pushing of self-interest. How can we learn to bring to social problems the same kind of open-minded attitude we bring to technical problems?

One theme of this book is that culture is a tool kit, and that we should learn to use it as we learn to use any other tool. But it is a tool with a difference because it sometimes has a mind of its own. Yet even an improperly understood screwdriver (and I have done fieldwork with people who didn't understand screwdrivers, for all that they learned very rapidly when screwdrivers were explained to them) either is useless or it causes havoc.

The first thing we have to fix, thus, is our attitude toward cultural matters. Our idea that social and cultural factors are just "natural" and drag along after technological change must be challenged. We can, to a degree, learn to use simulations to detect traps set by our tools. The fact that we may never be able to find all of the traps should make us wary, but should not make us turn our backs on the search. Simulation, if we can learn to use it, is a way of recontexting so that we can see some of the things our tools will do for us, and some of the ways they may turn on us, before we have to put them to the test.

Chapter 14

Some Lock-ins

H uman history is full of cultural traps; some of them have led to lock-ins. A lock-in is a cultural trap from which escape is impossible without immense insight and innovation. I am going to examine briefly three kinds of lock-ins.

Traps result when bodily adjustments made in aeons past, to conditions of that past, are blindly retained. Much has been written about the difficulty of reshaping the goals and attitudes of human males that were evolutionarily developed in response to the needs of getting a living by hunting. Much has also been written about differences between male and female proclivities in sex and childrearing—proclivities left over from earlier evolutionary adjustments. This type may be called the "old-hunter" lock-in.

The second kind—the "let-George-do-it" lock-in—results when new and perhaps ill-fitting responsibilities are piled onto existing institutions.

Finally, still other lock-ins arise when people are unwilling to examine the basic, out-of-awareness premises that underlie their culture, and hence insist on maintaining or even promoting cultural values that have come to be out of sync with the world they are living in. These can be called the "God made it so" lock-ins.

THE "OLD-HUNTER" LOCK-IN

The "Old Hunter" lock-in springs from the fact that cultural traditions sometimes expand beyond the capacities and proclivities of the human animal that evolved under earlier, simpler conditions. The position of women (and, of course, of men) in a society is a case in point. Developed in one social situation, gender attitudes may harden into demands and unstated premises that define behavior between men and women narrowly long after the original social situation has been completely altered. Such cultural rigidity wastes talent and undermines human rights.

Take the problem of the stranger. Like most other animals, human beings have come, in the course of evolution, to distrust strangers. Rats detect strangers by smell—if an experimenter puts a rat that "smells wrong" into an ongoing social system, the interloper will be attacked. Any stranger who cannot be run out of the social group may be killed. Domestic cats do it—introduce a new kitten to your two tabbies, and you may have to protect the kitten—the stranger—from death.

What rats do with their sense of smell—detect and define strangers—human beings do (or at least refine) with culture. People whose culture is different from our own are suspect. Indeed, threatening. We feel the cultural differences by sensing "incorrect" rhythms or nuances of language or habits. Our feeling is physical, just as the smell is physical to rats. We sometimes even use an analogy to smell in describing our sensing of difference. In reaction, people distance those who are culturally marked as strangers.

Some hunting-and-gathering societies define strangers into the same category as enemies. That was probably, at some time in the course of human development, an advantage in the survival game. Yet people moved from place to place and from one group to another in all hunting and gathering societies of which we have records. Women changed groups at marriage. (In a few places and times men moved to their wives' groups, but that was rare because it disrupted the ongoing organization of hunting groups.) An outcast or malcontent in one group might even gradually work his way into another if he did not first die alone in exile.

The way people dealt with strangers became more complex

when the Agricultural Revolution led to larger, more settled communities. In those larger groups, people could no longer know everybody in the community first hand. In small hunting and gathering communities there is little distinction between intimates and acquaintances. But with agriculture and the larger settlements it brought, intimates and strangers could be put on the same scale—some were now more strange than others. The stranger had become a part of life. But the inherited tendency to avoid strangers lived on.

As we move toward global society, the role of strangers has vastly enlarged—and will enlarge more. We can no longer distrust *all* strangers. But then, we can't trust them either. The fear is palpable: "they" may destroy "us."

In the United States today, there is considerable concern about the human rights of people who are "different"; men and women; heterosexual and homosexual people; differences in national origin, language groups and language barriers, religion.

Yet in American society, most immigrants—at least those from Europe—can become nonstrangers. It is traditional American wisdom that the full process of turning immigrants into Americans takes three generations. The stereotype says that the first generation is "displaced"; they dwell on the idea that the cultural tradition they brought with them is worthy of being passed on. Yet they feel that their tradition is being rejected—it is, after all, out of phase with the new cultural tradition in which they are immersed. Some aspects of the two traditions may not commingle comfortably. Furthermore, there is usually no help—and there may be active opposition—from the external community in passing on the old cultural tradition. In response, they may set up schools specifically to preserve ancestral culture—after-school schools to teach Chinese, or Judaism, or whatever the tradition that is being "preserved."

The second generation is likely to turn its back on this parental tradition and to concentrate instead on establishing an identity as performers of the accepted "greater" tradition that surrounds them, unmarked by the differences implied by the cultural tradition of their parents.

The third generation is, in a sense, born free—at least free enough to be curious about their "roots." The third generation are not strangers in the surrounding culture—unless, of course, race or other cultural assignment keeps them defined as strangers.

Not all societies allow strangers to become members—newcomers may be permanently marginalized. Japan is such a case. Though the Japanese are hospitable to whatever strangers they define as guests, they do not allow guests to "join the club." Some immigrants cease to be guests—and, if they cannot become members, become pariahs. Chinese immigrants, undetectable by racial criteria, are kept marginalized in Japan for many generations. Koreans, too, are never allowed to "become Japanese" even after their knowledge of Japanese language and culture is perfect.

Some strangers, in the United States at least, are turned into American ethnics. The boundaries of ethnicity are difficult to define, for all their cultural importance. Those ethnic groups may be turned into a hierarchy, not only of power but of regard.

In the global society that is emerging, in which people move about readily, almost everybody is a stranger almost everywhere. That is the reason why small local and kinship groups—groups of nonstrangers—are being reinforced even as global groups and special interest networks are expanding dramatically. Witness, for example, the phenomenon of support groups that has exploded in the United States. In one set of contexts, we are learning to behave well even as we remain strangers. But we still want to relax among people with whom we are not strangers.

Just as a scale for evaluating strangers—their degrees of strangeness—was established after the Agricultural Revolution, so now a more elaborate scale allows classification into many categories: enemies, allies, neutrals, alien nationalities. But the trap is closing as ethnicity emerges worldwide—consider Yugoslavia, or the former Soviet Union, or Africa, or southern Asia.

Traditionally, strong states have kept ethnic strife under some kind of control. But the powers of states are being eroded. The state will not "wither away" any more than the family has. Nevertheless, its position in the global power structure is changing. Ethnicity is emerging as one of the major problems of the twenty-first century.

THE "LET-GEORGE-DO-IT" LOCK-IN

The "Let-George-Do-It" lock-in arises when institutions are asked to do too many jobs for which they are unprepared or unfitted. An institution is a group of people united and organized for a purpose; such groups have the cultural resources and know-how to give them a good chance of achieving the purpose. However, successful institutions may also turn into backup institutions. In the same way that biological traits can freeload on successful genetic adaptations, so developing problems can freeload on successful cultural adaptations.

When change and development make a new need evident, some existing institution may step in or be pushed in to handle the new need. Such a backup institution must be basic, successful, and strong enough to bear the weight of "freeloaders." The family, the school, and the state are all basic and strong.

Using ordinary mammalian components, human beings developed the family, creating a special kind of organization. Over the years, cultural evaluations were attached to mammalian modes of reproduction and infant care, leaving us with such institutions as marriage and extended kinship networks. No other mammals have "families" in quite the human sense.

Human beings, having evolved into the family, *could* evolve out of it. Many tasks that people with simpler cultural traditions assign to the family have been stripped away from it in the industrial and postindustrial world and assigned to specialized institutions. Today about the only thing that the family can do that cannot be done by some other means is child rearing. If we can invent a "better" way to raise kids, the family *could* disappear. That is unlikely, however, because the family is an elegant institution: fewer people can do more for one another in families than within any other social form ever invented. Yet the purposes of the family have been seriously eroded as specialized institutions have stripped it of most of its economic and religious functions, its political and legal clout, its responsibility for the specifics of educating the young.

Yet, as family functions have been stripped away, family *responsibilities* have increased. Better said, family responsibilities have become more abstract. It is easy to teach a boy to shoot a bow and arrow—much harder to teach him how to go through school.

Families get a lot of lip service, but they don't get much support from other institutions in carrying out these abstract requirements. And nobody has yet figured out a practical, inexpensive way to go about providing that support. We all know that the family is a basic institution in every human society. We then tack on the premise that it *ought* to take the responsibility for everything that goes wrong with society—since character is formed in the family and since human inadequacy is defined as the result of inadequate upbringing. Because the family is the most generalized of the backup institutions, we tell ourselves that it *should* be able to do anything. Yet in its present context it can't do much of anything without society's support. Some people who know that perfectly well still rail about the inadequacy of the family instead of trying to improve the support system.

The school has a similar problem. Although schools have, in one sense, been around at least since the age of Plato and probably were there long before, schools free of religious doctrine that are intended to educate the entire public are only a little over 200 years old.

Today, just at the time that television and computers, multimedia technology and CD-Roms, are changing the nature of learning yet again, the schools have become a major backup institution. They have been handed the responsibility of socializing the young to a complex and changing world for the simple reason that adult family members can no longer know in detail all the things that their children must learn. Schools say that they want to avoid teaching morality; but they often do it and then blame the family because they have to do it. They try to prepare kids for jobs in the workplace—not to mention how to read and how to do addition and subtraction, how to keep well enough informed to vote intelligently, and how to balance a checkbook.

The schools have been invaded by assumptions from other cultural realms with demands that do not fit their organization. Teachers organized and became labor, which required that school boards and principals become management. No thought was given as to whether such an arrangement is a happy one for educational processes. I am *not* saying that the teachers and the school boards do not have just grievances. I am saying that their use of existing institutions to solve their problems, rather than creating new institutions that fit, may have made everybody's problems worse. But it may also be, of course, that we cannot create such new institutions until things break down.

Governments are seriously overburdened by nongovernment business. We live in a political age, in the same sense that the medieval period was a theological age. In the Middle Ages, all moral questions were referred to God, either directly or in the guise of His minions on Earth. Today, social problems that are not thrust either on the family or on the schools are handed to the government—the very while we complain that government is too big, costs too much, and does them badly. Problems whose solutions need a lot of money, or are concerned with emerging global society, or are central to the economy and the ecology—all are culturally defined as government problems. Government gets more and more mired in them.

People of industrial societies are used to having a powerful wraparound government, run as a highly specialized institution called the "state." Yet, governments existed long before there were states. Originally, governments were formed to do two basic political jobs: to settle disputes and keep the domestic peace on the one hand, and to maintain the integrity and safety of the social group against external enemies on the other.

The state, thus, is a specialized institution that emerged when social groups got so big that people could no longer govern themselves using kinship groups, religious congregations, and community. The state requires a kind of active leadership that is not necessary in nonstates. As governments are assigned additional tasks, more and more culture gets shoved into the realm of politics.

Governments, however, become unwieldy when social problems separate from the core political tasks are dumped on the state. The overburdened state cannot do all these extra tasks well, any more than the family can do everything assigned to it merely because there is nowhere else to assign the task. The state (and the market mechanism) cannot suitably address problems of the morality or immorality of social inequality, the welfare system, or impending ecological disaster.

Yet, there isn't, at the moment, any other way to do it. We must keep constantly in mind that today we need new kinds of social institutions to deal with the problems of today's global society— not to replace the old ones but to reinforce them by taking the "freeloader" issues off their backs.

When states developed to become nation-states, a new dimension of difficulty was added—the idea that the state should be associated with both a specific ethnic group and with a specific territory. The fact that almost no states were actually of that sort made no difference in creating the imaginary model. The idea appeared among the Portuguese in the fourteenth century. It logically leads to the proposition that the state should not only be associated with government, but should be the representative of what we today would call a dominant ethnic group, which should occupy and control its own territory. Its members become the only people with full rights within the territory.

That idea has been the plague of Europe ever since it appeared. From Portugal it migrated to Holland, Britain and France. The German idea of the *Volk* (fired by the ideas of the philosophical movement called German romanticism) means an ethnic group of people who look at themselves as something like a huge descent group with common ancestry, a common culture, and a common language—a "we" against all those "theys."

The state became "a culture." That idea was central to the peace processes at the end of World War I—by then it had become a basic premise of nationhood. Selfish nationalist ideas called "self-determination" emerged and grew. Personal identity and ethnocentrism were tied to the nation-state and confounded with patriotism. This association of the state with an ethnic group, and the whole being called a "nation," is one of the gravest cultural traps of modern times.

THE GOD-MADE-IT-SO LOCK-IN

The God-Made-It-So Lock-in grows out of the human need for morality. What is often overlooked is that human moralities throughout the world have a fascinating similarity beneath superficial differences. Yet most people examine their own moralities with too short a focal length. A short focal length throws the periphery into distortion, making the superficial differences seem bizarre or immoral. But if we can take a few steps back and encompass a broader field the distortion disappears. Focusing on a more extensive field makes the issues part of a larger whole. If we cannot take that step back, basic morality gets lost in a specific morality. The larger, more inclusive situation is left unserved.

This is not an argument in favor of "cultural relativism." I am not saying that everybody has a "right" to his or her own morality even if it means so confusing the society that it will no longer work. What I *am* saying is that people sometimes lock in on provincial problems to a degree that may be irrelevant or damaging to the species as a whole.

An example will help. When I was in West Africa, one of my assistants came back one evening from bathing in the river. He told me that someone had drowned there. When I asked who it was, he said it was a stranger who couldn't swim. When I asked if anybody had tried to save him, he responded that they had not. When I, in some agitation, asked if *he* hadn't tried to save him, he responded, "He wasn't mine." I have never been able to forget that incident. His cultural tradition had taught him to value the lives of his kinsmen and neighbors—people who were "his." My cultural tradition had taught me to value all human life. The focal length in my tradition was longer than his. But the ideas underlying the incident were the same: you help people. My tradition defined people differently from his.

Such a lack of phase between basic morality and provincial morality cannot be readily detected—a narrow definition of our own morality can blind us to the common principles that underlie all moralities. People cannot detect a greater morality because they are so rigidly trapped in the superficial aspects of their own delimiting definitions of morality and immorality.

Cultural traps and lock-ins abound. Better culture to help us recognize and counteract them is essential.

THE IDEOLOGICAL LOCK-IN

People, being capable of passionate belief—and sometimes prizing faith above reason—may compound their cultural traps and get locked into destructive patterns of action. When they do not allow themselves to examine and question the premises underlying their convictions they are likely to continue blindly, never considering where their actions might take them. When a significant portion of the people in a community share a set of irrational beliefs, their lock-ins take the form of ideologies. When an idealogy leads to such blindness, whether it is willful blindness or cowardly blindness, cults are likely to emerge.

An idealogy is a set of doctrines, assertions, and intentions that undergird a social, religious, or political position. Idealogies provide answers to eternal questions that allow the questions themselves to remain unasked: What is the nature of the good? the just? the beautiful? the right? When people do not allow themselves to question the traditional ideological answers, no matter what challenge they face, they stultify their capacities for psychological autonomy and self-determination. As they outlaw all questions—particularly those about the nature of human beings, power in human affairs, the nature of God, and the virtues of leaders—people are turning off their culturally informed animal capacities as feedback mechanisms. They are on the road to becoming automatons.

Communism is, for example, an idealogy that grew out of an honest search for amelioration of the inhumanities of early capitalism. One of its tenets was that if labor enters the same market as do goods, grave social injustices result. Marx's original vision of a better condition for all humanity was beautiful. Many people were so enamored of the vision that they would not allow themselves to notice the details of the political program that grew up around the vision. Some people ignored the sordid reality because they were concentrating only on the beauty and justice of the vision.

Liberalism is a group of idealogies—the word has meant many different things in the course of history. In the eighteenth century, liberalism was a Protestant movement that stressed free inquiry on the one hand and the ethical and humanitarian dimensions of Christianity on the other. It later became a political movement founded on the premises that human beings are basically good and sensible and that if they are adequately informed they would free themselves from destructive or arbitrary authority. If people were trained to—and allowed to—inquire into all aspects of their political and social lives, the information available to them would assure suitable decisions for the welfare of all. It's beautiful. Does it work?

Conservatism is an ideology that puts a brake on *all* culture change, in the conviction that any change may endanger what has already been achieved. It's comfortable. Does it work?

Fascism is an ideology that feeds on ethnocentrism and attacks the stranger—to the point of belligerent nationalism and racism. It claims that government should be centralized, under stringent economic controls, so that "inept" people (defined as strangers who lack the ability to look after their own welfare) would not be asked or allowed to make any decisions at all. Those controls seem seductive from one point of view—you don't have to take any responsibility for yourself. The price is that people put up with censorship and terrorism.

All the major world religions are beautiful visions of the nature of man and the kind of behavior and ritual required to bring that nature to its greatest flowering. But most of them—Buddhism may be an exception—can be twisted to support destructive political systems that undermine the ends toward which the religious vision claims to be reaching.

Feminism is an ideology—indeed, a whole raft of ideologies—based on the proposition that women should have equal social rank and rewards with men. As women have rethought their position and struggled to improve it, men have also been forced into reevaluating their own activities and premises. So far, both seem to have benefited, as perception has come into closer congruence with the new cultural context.

What all of these ideologies have in common is a vision of a beautiful world. Although the various visions differ in their details, all look forward to a world of plenty, of justice, of beauty, of harmony. The flaw is not in the vision. The difficulty comes, rather, when the vision blinds people to what is going on around them. When they cannot see the reality for the glare of the vision, that vision may become part of the problem instead of a solution.

The ease with which social science can be turned into ideology is frightening. There are, of course, social scientists who are dedicated Marxists. Insofar as that means that they study Marx's methods of reasoning or build on his many great insights, nobody can possibly object. But when they—or anybody else—put into their premises what ought to be in their hypotheses, we must begin to fear them and resist them. In precisely the same way, I know psychoanalysts (or at least I knew them some years ago) who take Freud's writings as gospel. It had become unspeakably bad social form, in their circles, to suggest that Freud was (like everybody else) a prisoner of his cultural tradition and of his era. They would not allow themselves to postulate that we should try to recast what was good about that past into a more current context, rather than just idealizing it. They define such an activity as presumptuous—which they express by saying that such people have not been adequately analyzed.

All this reminds one of the Ghost Dance. The Ghost Dance among Native Americans began in the late nineteenth century, as most of the Native American traditions were being destroyed by force. Starting in Nevada, the Ghost Dance spread throughout the Great Plains, the Great Basin, and to the Pacific Coast. Its premise was that if the Native American people would follow certain moral precepts and carry out specific rituals (which varied with the cultural tradition of the various groups into which these ideas were introduced), the ghosts of their dead ancestors would return, the White man would disappear, and everybody would live happily ever after. The dance was part of the ritual. They danced and danced—and nothing happened. Like all cults that hold out earthly promises that cannot be causally related to their rituals, this cult died out.

The oversimplifying cult with the beautiful vision is a freeloader on religion, be it on Native American religion or the so-called "religions of the Book"—Judaism, Christianity, and Islam. Cultism is a constant threat to religion. Established religions can espouse, or readily be turned into, political ideologies. They have only to use their platforms as blueprints for political action rather than as designs for moral living.

When ideologues demand that adherents either accept *all* their doctrinal points or else be branded as evil, their ideologies may become lock-ins—irreversible culture traps. If people's faith in their ideologies transcends their allegiance to law and organized religion, they are setting their course either toward chaos or toward their own collapse. That does *not* mean that people should not look for new visions or try to proselytize for them. It means, rather, that they should not lose touch with the contexts in which they live—that they should pay attention to the information that comes to them from the culture that is outside instead of only to the beautiful premises that are part of the culture within their heads. Even if they brand "reality" as immoral, people lose sight of it only at their own peril.

Ideologies are strong for the same reason that religions are strong: they give reassuring answers to at least some of the eternal questions. The lock-in occurs when the answer is considered of greater moment than the ability to question.

Ideologies differ from science (including social science) in that their propositions are not presented as theory to be criticized, tested, and improved, but rather as premises to be accepted on faith. All ideologies—all powerful faiths—must therefore be under constant surveillance, not to bring them down but to assure that any culture traps within them are recognized before they lead to lock-ins.

Religion provides many important comforts (which, for some people, may be necessities) that science cannot provide: solace in times of grief, the relief of admitting that some problems are greater than one's capacity to analyze them or even to bear them, trusting oneself to a higher power. However, as other theoretical explanations have developed, religion has become less and less an adequate explanation of the natural world. In that sense, it can become more and more a defense mechanism—and hence more and more of a trap. Yet when people need comfort more than they need factual and scientific explanation, religion comes into its own. Religion can, itself, become a lock-in because people need explanation of the unexplainable. The question becomes: How do people live with the cold comfort of real facts if they do not have the warmer comfort of community and reassurance? How do you more nearly separate "reality" from a learned cultural way of looking at reality?

Ideologies supply oversimplifications that allow people to deal with puzzling complexities within their cultural tradition. The danger comes when faith in the ideology lulls those people into banning inquiry. The growth of culture demands inquiry. Creativity is *based* on inquiry!

Science—including social science—lacks a built-in system of morality. There are standards of performance and honesty among scientists—fudging data or lying is a lapse serious enough to ruin careers. However, science is always guarded and controlled by moralities that come from outside it.

In our urge to explain and to find the security of good explanations, we must not give up our birthright of seeking better explanations. When we do, our cultural tradition becomes our enemy instead of our tool. We are locked in.

Your cultural tradition is like your language. The better you know it, the more you can understand and enjoy. But it is also like language in that it locks you into certain modes of thought and action. In *that* sense, every cultural tradition locks people in. The danger is that certain perturbations of it may lock them into a cauldron of destruction. The problem is—how do you detect the danger—and locate it?

Chapter 15

Visions and Scenarios

Cultural processes take place in time, developing from one action to another. They do not in themselves, however, have tenses—past, present, future. Actors in the process and observers of it—and the two may be the same—bring in the tenses.

Perceiving gives people an illusion of a present—the moment that is defined by perception. That "moment" allows either participants or observers to put some parts of the processes into the past and other parts into the future.

The present has no story because it has no time dimension. Just as a point may be a part of a line but have no dimension, so the present is a point in a process, perhaps many processes, but has no dimension.

What may be discerned as past can be turned into a story and called *history*—a complex word in English that means both what happened in the past and what later historians make of it. (The Chinese language, for one, is said not to have this problem.) Historiography is the exercises that historians perform to turn their interpretations of past events into a story.[1]

The future has proved more onerous. It can be turned into science fiction; if science fiction does not deny the laws of science as we know them—and especially if it does not spill over into the never-never land that its fans call fantasy—it can lead to entertaining and sometimes remarkably prescient stories.

However, organizing the future is more commonly a matter of visions and scenarios. Just here, English vocabulary begins to be a little shaky. A subject that is to the future what history is to the past still has no name, but it is developing among people who call themselves *futurists*. A method that is to the study of the future what historiography is to history can, if the neologism be allowed, be called *futurography*. Futurography is the exercise that futurists perform when examining probable futures as the cultural processes either continue or are changed by innovation, or as they suffer demolition.

Here we want to look at the complex idea of "history" and then at the even more complex idea of "futures"—the former complex because it has been thought about so much and because the word has so many meanings, the latter because it has been thought about comparatively little and its many meanings are confused for lack of clear definition.

HISTORY AND HISTORIOGRAPHY

The story of the past can be valued for many purposes. Some historians value the uniqueness of the individual situation and search out the story of each situation with no attempt to find patterns underlying that situation and others, similar to it, that have occurred in other places or other times. The story of the past can, however, be examined specifically in search of patterns that repeat themselves in different situations and in different ages. That is the goal of some social scientists as they study history.

Stories of the past can be created with or without a written record of past events, and with or without a discipline of historiography. In ancient China, where archives began in the Chou dynasty more than a thousand years B.C., court historians searched their archives so as to legitimize political and ritual activities. The premise was a Golden Age; it assumed that past ways were the right ways, and therefore one should look to the past for guidance about the future.[2] In nineteenth-century Africa, too, each family, clan, or community had a story to account for its origins; the story was sometimes used to provide guidance for the future. The Tiv of Nigeria, when I studied them in 1949–1953, had stories of their origins to their southeast; the stories focused on their migrations into their present territories and explained the juxtaposition of lineages on the ground, which was also an explanation of their political organization. They told and retold any one of some half-dozen standardized incidents to explain any variation from the geographical distribution that their genealogies posited as the correct one. Any of those incidents, with changeable characters, could be applied to any example of genealogical/geographic irregularity.

Indeed, the idea that all written histories should reflect "what really happened" came to be dominant in Europe only in recent centuries. The notion that the facts of history should comply with the records can be found earlier—indeed, there were unofficial histories in China that more or less followed this principle of "*wie es eigentlich gewesen*" and contradicted the official histories—but had not yet been elevated into doctrine. Anthropologists and historians, trying to reconstruct the history of places with no written records along lines acceptable to Western ideas of history, have had some success in separating "fact" from legend and myth in some African situations.

In short, history deals with dredging up whatever accounts of the past are available, reassessing them in terms of the historian's culture, then using them for purposes that are perceived in the present moment—one purpose may be illuminating the culture of the past time in which the events occurred. Thus history has two simultaneous time zones, so to speak: the time concurrent with the events and the time of the writer. The reader, too, brings a point of view based on his or her context—that makes three. Anyone who tries to read *The Decline and Fall of the Roman Empire* today knows that to make sense of it now, at the turn of the twenty-first century, a Roman time zone, Gibbon's time zone, and one's own time zone must all be considered.

The goal of many historians is to understand and report the culture of events at the time they occurred, keeping it strictly separate from their own time zone, and making sure that the latter does not intrude on the former. They call any lapse into anachronism by the (to them, insulting) term "presentistic."

The story of the future also has two focuses in time, but is different from history on most other counts. Since it cannot dredge up events that haven't yet happened, and since such unhappened events cannot be used to discover processes, studying futures works in almost an opposite way from studying history. Whereas history starts with events, futures start with the processes, then postulate likely events that will either maintain or upset those processes. The goal is to spell out a number of possible events that may allow continuation of the pattern, or to discern weak points in the pattern where either breakdowns or developments may occur.

For all that, however, the past is as much concocted by the historian as the future is by the futurist. "History" is turning events as we perceive them into story—and historiography is the set of principles for doing it. "Futures" is creating stories in the form of visions and scenarios, then looking for possibilities.

The other major differences between the exercises of historiography and those of futurography lie in the canons of proof for the events or processes that become part of the package. Just as the canons of scientific truth focus on methodology, so the canons for historiography focus on historians' canons of proof. Just so, futurography must focus on our knowledge of how culture works. Events of the past can be confirmed in written archives or archaeological discoveries, then turned into stories. Without some canons of confirmation, other historians may not accept them as history. Just so, continuing processes can be turned into all sorts of stories, but without principles of proof that the analysis of the pattern is "correct," they may not be acceptable.

In investigating the past, anthropologists may use either of two modes of approach. The first is called *ethnohistory*, a method in which ethnographers collect accounts from their informants about their past (too often with more or less contamination from the ethnographer's usually Western ideas of history—the contamination may well occur mostly in the rearranging or reordering of the parts). The resulting report of what they learn is called a people's view of their past. Ethnohistoriography—based on facts about the way a people examine events in their own past—has never been considered important enough to become a vital dimension of every ethnographic report. Although ethnographic examination of the past is not as underdeveloped as examination of the future, it nevertheless needs work.

The second mode of approach is to go beyond ethnohistory and abide by Western (or some other) rules of historiography—a set of premises that allows us to search for "what actually happened," as we excavate it from folklore.

In the same way, there are two modes of approach in understanding the future. One is called *ethnographic futures* by the man who invented it. Like historiography, ethnographic futures are built on facts. The facts, however, are not events from the past but rather statements that informants have made about probable futures that can be turned into scenarios. The second approach might be called futurography, although the people who practice it (*The Futurist* is their journal) do not use the word. They do, however, have certain principles for examining the future that can be seen as roughly equivalent to historiography when scholars examine the past. This second procedure can be called "running scenarios," reflecting the idea that every time an auspicious event occurs a whole new set of options opens up. We start from a specific, clearly indicated, place in the process, with known facts about how the process works; analysis of its weak points provides a guide to what is likely to change about it, and perhaps even provide some indication of specific changes.

FUTURES AND FUTUROGRAPHY

Futures are difficult because the kind of "facts" we use when we write the history of the future are not the kind of facts we use when we write the history of the past. Many people say there are no "facts" about the future. That may be a complication, but an even greater difficulty springs from the cultural tradition of social science, in which several premises stand in the way of our looking at what facts there are about the future. These anti-future arguments are true—and all are clichés that can blind us from looking beyond them. Yet, examining such clichés can clear the air. Here are three of many:

1. Specific events cannot be foretold. True.
2. Details about specific acts of creating the culture that will

change a pattern cannot always be anticipated. True, as long
as the "always" is kept in there.
3. The context of cultural activities can never be held constant
(as the context of chemistry experiments can). True.

And all are irrelevant.

Ethnographic Futures. As long as ethnographers fail to look at the
ideas people hold about the future, they are not doing their jobs
adequately. We can no longer merely announce that knowing
anything about the future is impossible because it hasn't happened yet. All ordinary people think about the future. They predict likelihoods whenever they make plans. Even very old people
(whose futures are necessarily foreshortened) act to insure that
things turn out the way they want them to turn out. Ideas about
the future are part of every ethnographic situation whether
ethnographers collect them or not.

People can look at the future with visions, but they may also
look at it as scenarios. A *vision* is said by the dictionaries to be a
mental image produced by the imagination—that may even have
a mystical or supernatural dimension. The dictionaries I consulted seem not to acknowledge that the word *vision* is also used in
today's political world to indicate a clearly communicated set of
goals for the future.

A scenario, on the other hand, is a model of an expected
sequence of events. Visions are based on hope. Scenarios are
based on knowledge (sometimes intuitive, which makes the distinction fuzzy) of cultural process.

Robert B. Textor has worked out a technique for studying possible future states that he calls "ethnographic futures research"—
ethnographic because his formulations are based on data from
informants in the best tradition of ethnographic reporting. He
asks people to examine the likely course of future events, then
helps them formalize what they have examined into a most desirable scenario (which, of course, reflects their hopes), a least desirable scenario (which reflects their fears), and finally a most
probable scenario. He has built a meticulous method for insuring
that his own ideas and premises do not color their responses.

Textor discovered that in the course of creating scenarios about
their futures, people fall back on—and hence reveal—their basic

values. Their hopes and their fears also reveal the fundamental action chains that they traditionally use to deal with challenges and problems. When such people act, they act in such a way as to bring about the situations they predicted—they cooperate to assure a self-fulfilling prophecy.

Ethnographic Futures Research is not a system for foretelling the future. It is, rather, a way of understanding that people project some of the elements of their current lives into the future, including their intentions to make things better. They plan at least some of the ways their lives and their cultural tradition might profitably be changed.[3]

A scenario produced by Textor's method is better thought out than one produced in other ways. As his informants work, they (not purposely or even consciously) use the entire arc of culture that is available to them—local, national, global, religious, technical—instead of merely some portion of it excised to provide special identities, such as ethnic culture. When informants analyze their own cultural traditions, they have entered a new and productive realm. At least some of the lurking premises of the culture are exposed. There is no aspect of the context that is not called into play.

Running Scenarios. History does not, of course, repeat itself. But cultural patterns do. This again brings up the age-old problem of comparison.[4]

A running scenario does not deal with the likelihood of future conditions based on ethnographic accounts, but rather with options that are altered as cultural processes proceed, and as purpose either persists or changes through many historical vicissitudes. Instead of informants' scenarios of probable events, analysts have to create ways of maintaining running scenarios as we look at choice-making in processes that began in the past and will continue into the future.

What options does seeing processes-in-context provide to the people who live there? What new choices result when one of these options, rather than the others, is acted on? What are the bases for the choices that real people actually make?

We can thereupon look at problems within any specific cultural tradition not only in the light of its historical record, but also from the standpoint of similar situations in other traditions—that anthropological stock in trade, the comparative method. Only when we know what other peoples in the historical and the ethnographic records have done in similar circumstances (and also take into account ethnographic futures scenarios) can we begin to make educated running scenarios, and from them plans. Such running scenarios are a form of knowledge about the processes and where they will likely go from here.

When we examine any processual pattern, we are at the same time examining answers contained within that pattern as to how one cultural tradition or another has dealt with problems like those we are currently facing. We can thereupon sharpen our judgment about the range of possibilities—and, in particular, the impossibilities.

With such data about cultural processes, anthropologists can prepare this second kind of scenario. Preparing scenarios with our premises as fully overt as we can make them—and understood as well as we can manage—allows us to examine at least *some* of the culture traps that have shown up in different avatars of the process. Does it really appear that people have come to the point where they can overcome the problems *this* time around a cycling pattern? Have they at least figured out some of the things they should *not* do? Or are they running on blind hope? That kind of hope kills.

When anthropologists recontext answers from many cultural traditions into anthropological culture, they must take note of the fact that the new context may alter the situation utterly. The "fact" that the French solved such-and-such a problem in a certain way in the seventeenth century may not mean in anthropological culture what it meant in seventeenth-century French culture: additions and subtractions and warpings probably accompany any recontexting. It *certainly* does not mean that another people, say the Canary Islanders in the early twenty-first century, can do it that way. And it certainly does not mean that the theoretical base of anthropology will not shift and change with anthropological successes and their contexts, thus dating our insights.

Nevertheless, anthropologists and historians have amassed a warehouse full of solutions—the ways that many peoples from many places and many times have solved problems. If the cultural patterns to be found in that warehouse can be analyzed and computerized, a whole new world could open up. What we are lacking right now is ways to index such human experiences—ways like turning "heat" into "temperature," which allows new kinds of measurement and comparison. First understand them in context, and then compare them at the level of process.

The lack is not in the data. Rather it is in our skill in devising comparative categories that accommodate the data and make sense of it. It is a theoretical problem much more than it is a field-work problem. The trap, however, is before us: it is easy to derive such categories from events in our own current world—turning our own folk ideas into theories for judging the rest of the world. That way blinds us to the possibility that some discoverable (but not currently available) way of *looking* at our problems may make them readily soluble.

We *can* learn to play this difficult process game. But it takes discipline and a lot of will and courage. Bill Powers (who wrote *Behavior, the Control of Perception*)[5] once invented a game something like chess, but in which every move not only changed the juxtaposition of the pieces on the board but also changed the state of the board on which the game was being played. That is what cultural process does. His game taught a valuable lesson, but was too disquieting (and perhaps too complex) to engage very many people. The fluid rules were too much like real life—people prefer games (and theories) that limit the range of relevance and pin down all the rules.

Stories change with the context in which they are told. The pattern remains. But nobody knows very much about the introduction of new patterns, for which new kinds of stories are demanded. There is a constant feedback between the story process and the context of the story. Simulations are also dependent on context. They must change as values change—and as events alter the game board. A simulation is good for what it is good for, but its usefulness disappears (or is at least reduced) with changes in the situations it was designed to illuminate.

And so with futures: the future is dependent on perceptions in the present, as is any view of the past. And yet the present is an illusion between past and future. Thinking about the future is full of the gravest culture traps, and also possibilities of disaster from outside the system. Thinking about the past is also full of traps, but those traps would seem to have less immediate impact, especially if we can learn that the past may *not* be an adequate guide to the future. In classical Chinese tradition, and to a lesser degree in every other, a vision of the past dictated action for the future. We have at least got to the place where we can examine the past as an example of the process rather than use it blindly as a guide into the "unknown."

Anthropological futures means, first of all, placing ourselves *in* the process, then understanding it well enough to anticipate it more cogently. Difficulties arise from innovations, the crumpling of the control space, and disasters that originate outside the system. Anthropology *can*, however, analyze weaknesses in the process that we want to avoid or weed out, as well as the strengths that we want to keep or build up. Doing that becomes a matter of policy.

Vision grows not out of hope, but out of the process of analyzing cultural processes, particularly grasping the importance of premises. Anyone who can see the premises of his or her culture, question them at the right time, and replace them whenever it is necessary—that is vision.

It can be said in a flowchart:

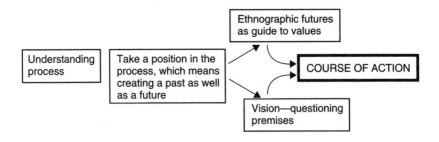

This is, of course, an exercise that skillful managers and statesmen engage in everyday. They try to focus on process and on future states at the same time. They need both ethnographic futures scenarios to get their associates organized toward a commonly perceived set of working goals, and running scenarios so they can figure out how they might use the process to get there from here.

———————

This book is full of unanswered questions—but questions are more fruitful than answers, which have a way of stopping inquiry in its tracks. The history of anthropology, like the history of all social science, involves first discovering questions and then making them obsolete, sometimes with answers, but more often with better questions. It's the most exciting game in the universe. Fortunately. Because it is the only one.

NOTES

Road Map

1. The verb *to cultivate*, which is etymologically the sensible verb, has been used up. Using it in the present context would create what William Empson has called a "negative pregnancy," trying to make a word mean less than, or something different from, what the ordinary reader knows perfectly well it means. You can sometimes make a word mean more than it ever meant before, but almost nobody has ever been successful in making a word mean less than it meant before.

2. Arnold Van Gennep, *The Rites of Passage*, 1908, translated by Monika B. Vizedom and Gabrielle L. Caffee, introduction by Solon T. Kimball (Chicago: University of Chicago Press, 1960).

3. Victor Turner, *Schism and Continuity in an African Society: A Study of Ndembu Village Life* (Manchester: Manchester University Press/Rhodes-Livingstone Institute, 1957).

4. Paul Bohannan, *Justice and Judgment Among the Tiv.* (London: Oxford University Press/International African Institute, 1957). Reissue by Waveland Press, 1989.

5. Michael Thompson, *Rubbish Theory.* (London, Oxford University Press, 1979).

6. Paul Bohannan, "Some Models for Planning the Future," *Journal of Social and Biological Structures* 7:1 (1984), 37–59.

7. John Platt, "Social Traps," *American Psychologist* 28:8 (1973), 641–51.

8. Jules Henry was onto this same kind of issue as early as 1963 in *Culture Against Man* (New York: Random House, 1963).

Chapter 1. Matter, Life, and Culture

1. A. L. Kroeber, "The Superorganic," *American Anthropologist* 19 (1917). He assigns the creation of the word *superorganic* to Herbert Spencer, but notes that Spencer's use of the word was such as to indicate that the problems of Spencer's day were quite different from those of Kroeber's.
2. William T. Powers, *Behavior: The Control of Perception* (Chicago: Aldine Press, 1973).

Chapter 2. A Model of the Human Animal

1. A good summary of behaviorism, based on stimulus-response, is to be found in Morton Hunt, *The Story of Psychology* (New York: Doubleday, 1993), pp. 242–79. Hunt's recounting the lives of prominent behaviorists adds interest.
2. William T. Powers, *Behavior: The Control of Perception* (Chicago: Aldine Press, 1973).
3. Ronald W. Casson, "Schemata in Cognitive Anthropology," *Annual Review of Anthropology* 12 (1983), 429–62.

Chapter 3. What Culture Does to Society I: Culturized Animal Behavior

1. At some point, associated with size and maybe some other factors, the quality in this compound dyad changes: the "relationship" between a person and the state of which he is a citizen stretches this point, because the feedback from individual to state is limited.
2. Other people may add other principles as they gain new insights, or make finer distinctions, or as our views of society become more refined. The number is not important. Understanding how each principle works and the grounds on which it differs from other principles *is* important.
3. Edward T. Hall, *The Hidden Dimension* (New York: Doubleday, 1965).
4. American and European anthropologists have traditionally begun the discussion of kinship either with kinship terminology or with sexuality rather than with shared genes. That emphasis comes not only from the fact of the priority of sexuality in any single reproduction cycle; it is also a product of the prejudices of their own cultures.
5. Anthropologists in the past have argued about whether what they study as kinship is biological or purely cultural. Such arguments

seem to me to miss the point: kinship is a biological phenomenon, but in the process of culturization the biology involved can be almost blotted out of people's concern.

6. This statement is not meant to deny differences between men and women. Rather, it is an exhibit about the differences between sex and gender. In complex culture, the sex of the person matters less and less. However, the *gender* of the person may be determining. Developed cultures have mechanized "labor" to the extent that its divisions *per se* have little to do with sex differences but a lot to do with culturally defined gender differences.

7. Cooperation may indeed be one of the bases of harmony, but complete harmony is a state of utopia; all aggressive action disappears. The human urge to reduce tension may lead to the error of enshrining cooperation as the key to a "nicer" society. This can be dangerous, leading to erosion of individual rights.

8. Robert Axelrod and William D. Hamilton, "The Evolution of Cooperation." *Science*, 211 (1981):1390–96.

Chapter 4. What Culture Does to Society II: Human Social Organization

1. Many anthropologists (erroneously, I think) deny or ignore the biological dimension, which allows them to dismiss this problem. It becomes what Michael Thompson would call an excluded monster; it will either hold up the progress of the discipline or make those particular anthropologists irrelevant—or both.

2. The numbering continues the numbering in Chapter 3.

3. Henry Sumner Maine, *Ancient Law: Its Connection with the Early History of Ideas, and Its Relation to Modern Ideas*.

4. Karl Polanyi *The Great Transformation* (New York: Holt, Rinehart and Winston, 1944).

Part II. Cultural Dynamics

1. An earlier version of portions of this Part were published as "Some Models for Planning the Future," *Journal of Social and Biological Structures* 7:1 (1984), 37–59. My thinking at that stage owed a great deal to Harvey Wheeler, then editor of *JSBS*.

2. Robert Redfield, *The Folk Cultures of Yucatan* (Chicago: University of Chicago Press, 1944, 133).

Chapter 5. Chains: Trajectories and Cycles

1. The term *action chain* is Edward T. Hall's in *The Hidden Dimension* (Doubleday, 1966). I did not distinguish them from *event sequences* when I described the latter in *Justice and Judgment Among the Tiv* in 1957 and in *Social Anthropology* in 1963. Richard Schechner (*Between Theater and Anthropology*, University of Pennsylvania Press, 1985) uses the term *strips of culture* for action chains.

2. The -*s* appeared on the word *culture* early in the twentieth century because anthropologists needed such a term. It is unfortunate that the terminology developed as it did, because "culture" is the generic term, and "culture-to-which-an-s-can-be-added" is a specific form of it. When genus and species have the same name, confusion is likely to erupt. However, the usage has spread so far beyond anthropology into the general culture (in this case, the singular of cultures-with-an-s) that changing it by fiat, no matter how sensible, is probably impossible.

3. Edward T. Hall, *Beyond Culture* (New York: Anchor Press/Doubleday, 1977). See also his *The Dance of Life and other Dimensions of Time* (New York: Anchor Press/Doubleday, 1983), and pp. 24–25 of Edward T. Hall and Mildred Reed Hall, *Understanding Cultural Differences* (Intercultural Press, Inc., 1990).

4. Edward T. Hall, *The Hidden Dimension* (New York: Doubleday, 1966).

5. Victor Turner, *The Ritual Process: Structure and Anti-Structure* (Chicago: Aldine Publishing Co., 1969) called this state *limin* (a noun referring to the threshold, derived from the adjective *liminal*); Richard Schechner, op. cit., has called it *transformational*.

6. Margaret Mead made this point in *New Lives for Old* (New York: William Morrow, 1956), which is the earliest example I know of it.

7. Paul Bohannan, *Justice and Judgment among the Tiv* (London: Oxford University Press/International African Institute, 1957, p. 100), called it an "event sequence." That book is currently in print from Waveland Press.

8. Victor Turner, *Schism and Continuity in an African Society* (Manchester: Manchester University Press, 1957).

9. Michael Thompson, *Rubbish Theory* (Oxford: Oxford University Press, 1979, 135–36).

10. Frederik Barth, editor, *Ethnic Groups and Boundaries.* (Boston: Little Brown, 1966, p. 4).

11. When I studied the Tiv in 1949–53 they numbered about 800,000 people. In 1994 there were over three million of them. I would like to know what has happened to those rubbish ancestors in the processes of population growth. Either the genealogies are deeper than they were, or else their areas of relevance have been vastly decreased, or else—least likely—some of those rubbish ancestors have been resuscitated.

Chapter 6. Transformation and Recontexting

1. Scholars like Kai Erikson in *A New Species of Trouble* (New York: Norton, 1994, especially pp. 141–43) distinguish technological disasters from natural disasters. The results of some industrial accidents do indeed lead to disaster (as Chernobyl and Bhopal illustrate); they are likely to be, in cultural impact, more like physical disaster than like social disaster.
2. A good summary of Chomsky's progress is P. H. Matthews' "Language as a Mental Faculty" in N. E. Collinge, ed., *An Encyclopedia of Language* (London: Routledge, 1990), pp. 112–38.
3. Benjamin L. Whorf, *Language, Thought and Reality* (New York: Wiley, 1956).
4. V. Propp (Vladimir Iakovlevich), *The Morphology of the Folk Tale* (Austin: University of Texas Press, 1968). The original Russian was published in 1928; the original English translation (of which this is said to be an improved edition) was published in 1956.
5. Paul Bohannan, *Justice and Judgment among the Tiv* (London: Oxford University Press/The International African Institute, 1957).
6. One of Ruth Benedict's lasting contributions to anthropology—it dominates all her work—was to discern and illuminate such dominating ideas in a cultural tradition, which she then called "patterns." Some of her details seem wrong-headed today, but the principle remains a beacon.
7. K. Groos, *The Play of Animals* (New York: Appleton, 1898).
8. Donald Symons, *Play and Aggression: A Study of Rhesus Monkeys* (New York: Columbia University Press, 1978).
9. George E. Schaller, *The Serengeti Lion: A Study of Predator–Prey Relationships* (Chicago and London: University of Chicago Press, 1972). See especially pages 156–159.
10. Gregory Bateson, *Steps Toward an Ecology of Mind* (Novato, CA: Chandler Publishing Co., 1972). See especially page 179.

Chapter 7. Pattern and Turbulence

1. Vladimir Propp, *The Morphology of the Folk Tale* (Austin: University of Texas Press, 1968). The original Russian was published in 1928; the original English translation (of which this is an improved edition) was published in 1956.

2. Ruth Benedict, *Patterns of Culture* (Boston: Houghton Mifflin, 1934).

3. Emile Durkheim, *Suicide* (Glencoe, IL: Free Press, 1951). The original French was published in 1897.

4. Michael Thompson, *Rubbish Theory* (London: Oxford University Press, 1979).

5. C. H. Waddington, *Tools for Thought* (New York: Basic Books, 1977).

6. René Thom, *Stabilité Structurelle et Morphogénèse* (Paris: Benjamin, 1972). Thom's work has been criticized, even dismissed, by some mathematicians. The models that follow here are not mathematical, as far as I know.

7. William Empson, in *The Structure of Complex Words* (London: Chatto & Windus, 1951), demonstrated how people can pack many different meanings into a single word, then hop among the meanings, giving themselves the impression they are not changing the subject. The same kind of thing happens when different ideas are packed into what appear to be single concepts. We can hop among the ideas without ever examining their different meanings.

8. To put it into terms I have used elsewhere (Paul Bohannan, *Social Anthropology* [New York: Holt, Rinehart and Winston, 1963] and Paul Bohannan, *We the Alien* (Prospect Heights, IL: Waveland Press, 1991), everything was handled by a bicentric mode, the way we handle foreign affairs; none by a unicentric mode of state political organization, which implies an organizationally complex monolith.

9. *Responsibility* is a very Western concept. You can, of course, say it in African languages, but the burden it bears in those languages is very different from the burden it bears in English or French.

10. When I studied the Tiv in 1949–1953, they numbered somewhat less than 800,000. By 1993, their number had exceeded 3,000,000.

11. *Tsav* is a physical substance that attaches to the heart, which I have seen, since Tiv often performed postmortem examination to discover whether it was present. It looks to me like sacs of blood in the pericardium. I have never been able to get a doctor to tell me what it is without first seeing it.

12. Paul Bohannan, "Extra-processual Events in Tiv Political Institutions," *American Anthropologist* 60:1–12, 1958.
13. Michael Thompson, *Rubbish Theory* (Oxford: Oxford University Press, 1979:183). The quotation following is on page 84.

Chapter 8. What Culture Change Involves

1. Robert B. Edgerton, *Sick Societies: Challenging the Myth of Primitive Harmony* (New York: Free Press, 1992).

Chapter 9. Innovations and Cultural Cusps

1. Writing clearly and simply can also turn profound insights into obviousnesses, thus creating a challenge to both writer and reader.
2. U.S. Kerner Commission, *The Kerner Report: The 1968 Report of the National Advisory Commission on Civil Disorders* (New York: Pantheon Books, 1968; paperback, Bantam Books, New York, 1968).

Chapter 10. Disasters and Cultural Traps

1. Kai Erikson, *A New Species of Trouble* (New York: Norton, 1994).
2. See *Alaska Geographic* 1972:31.
3. Claus-M. Naske, and Herman E. Slotnick, *Alaska: a History of the 49th State*, (Norman: University of Oklahoma Press, 1987), p. 179.
4. Bruce Porter, *War and the Rise of the State* (New York: Free Press, 1994).
5. Anthony F. C. Wallace, "Psychological Preparation for War," in Morton Fried, Marvin Harris and Robert Murphy, *War: The Anthropology of Armed Conflict and Aggression* (New York: Natural History Press, 1968).
6. Edward T. Spicer, ed., *Perspectives in American Indian Culture Change* (Chicago: University of Chicago Press, 1961). Despite its age, this remains the best single source on the subject.
7. Gordon L. Pullar, "Ethnic Identity, Cultural Pride, and Generations of Baggage: A Personal Experience." *Arctic Anthropology* 29:2, 182–191.
   Harold Napoleon, "Yu'yu'raq: the Way of Being Human." Unpublished manuscript.

Chapter 11. Cultural Dissonance

1. As far as I know, Leon Festinger, in *A Theory of Cognitive Dissonance* (Evanston, IL: Row Peterson, 1957), introduced the idea of cogni-

tive dissonance into behavioral science. But it is undoubtedly older.

2. Paul Bohannan, *Social Anthropology* (New York: Holt, Rinehart and Winston, 1963).

Chapter 12. Beyond Fieldwork

1. Edmund Wilson, in *To the Finland Station* (originally published in 1940; I consulted the 1972 edition—New York: Farrar, Straus and Giroux) provides good examples of the way that the likes of Saint-Simon and Robert Owen proceeded along lines of action without ever knowing that they did not understand the reason for their failures or successes. It lay partly in the fact that they had no data and no idea about how either organizations or people worked.

2. Vladimir Propp, *The Morphology of the Folk Tale* (Austin: University of Texas Press, 1968). The original Russian was published in 1928; the original English translation (of which this is said to be an "improved edition") appeared in 1956.

3. He has been unmercifully (and unfairly) criticized by scholars who claim that his structures do not exhaust the possible structures of folk tales or that his particular structures are not universal. Instead of understanding the importance of pattern to story and proceeding to unearth other patterns for stories that the Propp patterns do not fit—that is, going to a generic level rather than being stuck at the specific—these critics have contented themselves with bad-mouthing Propp. This is the essence of the methods of third-rate intellectuals.

4. For more detail see Paul Bohannan, "Tiv Divination," in J. H. M. Beattie and R. G. Lienhardt, editors, *Essays in Memory of E. E. Evans-Pritchard by his Oxford Colleagues* (Oxford: Clarendon Press, 1975).

5. I may be wrong about this. Are storyteller and audience actually lacking in our daily lives?

Chapter 13. Simulation

1. Secretary of State Warren Christopher, in an interview on the Mac-Neil-Lehrer News Hour on December 17, 1993, carefully made the distinction between market-dominated economy and democracy-dominated polity. However, his *policy* was *not* to distinguish them for action purposes. Rather, the policy was purposefully to associate them. The question, "Are they really inevitably tied to each other?"

was recognized but avoided. He was loyal to his side but in the process he funked the larger issue: how do you avoid the tragic aspects of the free market at the same time that you avoid the tragic aspects of a controlled polity?

2. It is interesting that, in the last couple of years, anthropologists have begun to pick up the glove thrown down in 1963 by Jules Henry in his brilliant but ahead-of-its-time book, *Culture Against Man* (New York: Random House). Indications that anthropologists are beginning to exercise themselves with what is wrong with cultures can be found in Robert Edgerton's *Sick Societies* (New York: Free Press, 1992) and in Clifford Geertz's book review, "Life on the Edge" (*New York Review of Books*, April 7, 1994, pp. 3–4).

Chapter 15. Visions and Scenarios

1. Some historians have tried to adopt the rules of generalization that they attribute to physical science. They have not been signally successful.

2. The articles under "Historiography" in the *Encyclopedia of the Social Sciences* (New York: The Macmillan Company and The Free Press, 1968) are interesting concerning these matters.

3. Sippanondha Ketudat, *The Middle Path for the Future of Thailand: Technology and Harmony With Culture and Environment*, with the methodological and editorial collaboration of Robert B. Textor (Honolulu and Chiang Mai: Institute of Culture and Communication, East-West Center, 1990). See also Robert B. Textor, "A Brief Explanation of Ethnographic Futures Research," *Anthropology Newsletter*, November, 1989.

4. Murray J. Leaf, *Man, Mind and Science: a History of Anthropology* (New York: Columbia University Press, 1979). See especially Chapter 5.

5. William T. Powers, *Behavior: The Control of Perception* (Chicago: Aldine Press, 1973).

Acknowledgments

It is hard to know where to start when I consider the people who have been instrumental in my study of cultural process—and even harder to know where to stop. If I tried to be inclusive, I would almost surely inadvertantly leave out important people. Therefore I mention only a few high points. Because I have been at this topic at least since the late 1940s, I'd better begin with Edward Spicer, from whom I learned a great deal and whose work I greatly admire—Ned understood the importance of time, did extensive historical research, and would have encouraged this effort. It also owes a lot to E. E. Evans-Pritchard, who was first my mentor, then my boss and close friend during the years I spent in Oxford. Whenever I reread him I realize "So *that* is where I learned that!" As I remember, it was Clyde Mitchell who insisted so often that I study van Gennep's *Rites of Passage* that I finally did it.

More recently, I want especially to thank Harvey Wheeler, who was a major influence during the late 1970s and early 1980s. Harvey knows a lot about an awful lot of things; talking with him was always an instructive delight. When he was editor of *The Journal of Social and Biological Structures*, he published an early version of some of the ideas in this book.

Finally, I cannot omit John Platt, whom I had long known but got to know well when we were colleagues in the University of California, Santa Barbara, from about 1976 to 1982; Edward T. Hall, whose ideas permeate the book; and Robert Textor, who not only read the entire manuscript but has also helped me get through a lot of futures. Robin Fox was immensely helpful with early versions of this book.

Bruce Nichols at The Free Press insisted magnificently that I get it all in and get it in the right order; Camilla Hewitt copyedited the book and, bless her, made it look as if I am better than I probably am.

Index

211